KARPOV
— ON —
KARPOV

MEMOIRS OF A CHESS WORLD CHAMPION

KARPOV
— ON —
KARPOV

MEMOIRS OF A
CHESS WORLD CHAMPION
ANATOLY KARPOV

Translated from the Russian by
Todd Bludeau

ATHENEUM
New York 1991

MAXWELL MACMILLAN CANADA
Toronto

MAXWELL MACMILLAN INTERNATIONAL
New York   Oxford   Singapore   Sydney

Copyright © 1990 by Liberty Publishing House, Inc.

English translation copyright © 1991 by Macmillan Publishing Company, a division of Macmillan, Inc.

Atheneum
Macmillan Publishing Company
866 Third Avenue, New York, NY 10022

Maxwell Macmillan Canada, Inc.
1200 Eglinton Avenue East, Suite 200
Don Mills, Ontario M3C 3N1

Library of Congress Cataloging-in-Publication Data

Karpov, Anatoly, date.
    Karpov on Karpov : memoirs of a chess world champion / Anatoly Karpov ; translated from the Russian by Todd Bludeau.
        p.   cm.
    Simultaneously published in Russian.
    Includes index.
    ISBN 0-689-12060-5
    1. Karpov, Anatoly, date.   I. Title.
    GV1439.K37A3   1991   91-16031 CIP
    794.1'092—dc20
    [B]

Macmillan books are available at special discounts for bulk purchases for sales promotions, premiums, fund-raising, or educational use. For details contact:

              Special Sales Director
              Macmillan Publishing Company
              866 Third Avenue
              New York, NY 10022

10 9 8 7 6 5 4 3 2 1

Printed in the United States of America

"Sister mine, Caissa"

KARPOV
— ON —
KARPOV

MEMOIRS OF A CHESS WORLD CHAMPION

CHAPTER ONE

WHAT COULD I HAVE UNDERSTOOD THEN? Absolutely nothing. But I could distinguish good from evil. And these people gave off such evil that even I, a boy, was shocked. That is why, it seems, I remember everything, right down to the smallest detail.

I remember the white down floating through the room and the two bayonets flashing in the corners of the room. I am sure that this is my own memory, that it does not come from the stories my father, mother, and sister, Larisa, told, because these images of the room—the down flocks, the clumsy men in heavy overcoats, the chest drawers pulled out, their contents overturned, and the books splayed under their shelves like broken fans—I remembered all this from three distinct angles. At first I must have observed the search from my bed, but when the investigator decided that it, too, had to be searched, my mother took me in her arms and stepped back between the windows. That was the second angle. Then, tired from holding me, she crossed the room to sit on the edge of the stripped bed, on the iron mesh—this was the third and final angle. I remember the mesh, how the nickel-plated spheres on the spine of the bed shone in my face.

Mama says they pounded on our door, alarming all our neighbors. I awoke to the harsh voice of the investigator. I don't know what my parents said, or whether the two soldiers ever uttered a word. But even now, the metallic knocking of their rifle butts rings in my ears, along with the thud of books thrown to the floor, and the scraping of furniture being jerked about.

The first days of 1953 passed. The weeks remaining to Stalin's death were numbered. To this day I still do not know who wrote the denunciation against my father, what "compromising material" they were searching for, and why, finally, they did not arrest him, even though no evidence was needed to make an arrest (evidence was fabricated during an investigation). I only know that we were lucky.

I grew up a homebody. When I say a "homebody," I mean that I was raised almost entirely at home. While the majority of urban Soviet children have to attend nursery school and kindergarten, I was spared—after I was born, Mama quit her job as economist at a factory to raise me and my sister, Larisa.

I was introduced to illness at an early age and grew accustomed to it. There is probably not one single childhood ailment I didn't contract, and some of them stuck with me for months. Had I undergone the severe nursery and kindergarten schools, with their obliteration of personal responsibility, their indifference, their enforced adherence to the principle of "do as everyone else does," their adherence to a culture of kitsch and cliché, and the struggle for everything—for a toy or a place in the clique, for praise from the teacher or attention from the group—had I experienced this, I'm convinced I would have turned out differently, more conforming and less independent, and I never would have achieved what I have. But I was fortunate. Mama decided that while we would be less well-off at home (her former salary had been the chief contribution to the family budget), she would raise her children the way *she* wanted. I am grateful to her for this courageous step.

I remember how my world expanded. At first it consisted only of our apartment. Then for two or three years, until I began school, it was confined to the boundaries of our courtyard. And then suddenly it burst open all at once, and my whole southern Urals town of Zlatoust became my world. We lived in a five-room communal apartment on the fourth floor. As was the norm in those days, the number of rooms defined the number of families. Our family was the largest, followed by two smaller families and, finally, two women who lived on their own. When I was four, one of the single women who lived on the other side of the wall from us moved out of her apartment, and we were permitted to take over her space. True, her room was tiny, but we were glad to have even a small chance to spread out. We made a door from our room into this attic room and walled up its former door. In this way we were at least able to have a separate apartment.

Here I must mention our balcony. Very few families had one in our building, and we were proud of ours. For me, it was like a springboard to the world outside. Swallows lived above the door on the balcony. They appeared every spring, completely unafraid of us. I fed them, but I was never able to tame one. This upset me

to the point of tears. "You're wrong," my father told me.
"For your small good deed—for a few crumbs—you
expect something in return. But by doing so you'll
destroy that good deed and turn it into a common
transaction."

"Didn't you teach me that everything has a price?"

"But you already got your payment, son. Think about
it: Why did you feed the birds? Because they were hun-
gry? No. It was simply because you wanted to. You
wanted to—they didn't ask for it. You did it, and you
were happy when you saw how they ate it."

"But I really want to . . ."

"If you really want to, then do something more for
them, think of something and do something really great
for them so that they'll believe in you, so that they'll
come to you themselves. But you gave them just a little
bit, and you want a great deal in exchange."

"For them to eat from my hand—that's a lot?"

"Of course! That's a huge payment. Essentially you
want them to give up their freedom to you for these
crumbs. It's the only thing they have."

"But sparrows eat from my hand."

"Sparrows are beggars. Learn to respect the freedom
of others. Look, you may still be young, but your mother
and I treat you like an adult, and we are attentive to
every one of your wishes. You should learn this rule:
Take into consideration every person you meet in life.
Better yet, take into consideration every living thing."

My father didn't think about my age. He spoke to me
as if I were an adult, convinced that it was never too
early to form a child's outlook on life, and he set an
example with his own behavior and actions. He knew

that eventually his words, like seeds dropped into a field, would take root.

Each autumn my father and I performed a ritual which I liked very much. At the first signs of frost we walked to the Gromotukha to gather large stones which my father carried home in a knapsack. I enjoyed everything about these excursions: the planning, the walk to the stream, during which time we discussed my problems (as far as I remember, my father was always incredibly busy, and therefore we greatly valued every minute spent together), and the care with which we selected our stones, based on shape and weight. After Mama had carefully washed them off with soap, we then used these stones to hold down the lids of the oak barrels we used for pickling cabbage.

I knew deprivation from an early age. It had many faces—in food, clothing, domestic items, everything. But I wasn't aware of it, because everyone around us or whose apartments I visited lived exactly the same—some a little better, others a little worse. My parents' friends and the parents of my pals were all of the same circle, the same means, the same level of indigence. They all worked in metal factories or served in municipal offices. There wasn't a boss among them. In those days the war still sat firmly in our consciousness, and the custom of living with a tightly drawn belt, with thoughts foremost for the country and its business, had not changed. Of course, there weren't just poor people; we knew people with money and heard about the rich. But the stratification of society had only just commenced. The well-to-do and wealthy lived somewhere, but not near us. Riches were associated with an immoral way of life, with dishonest hands. The people of our circle were not ashamed of their poverty; on the contrary, they used it as an argument for self-justification: "My pockets are empty, but my conscience is clear."

Our deprivation was the product of two circumstances. First, Mama quit her job after my birth to take care of us children and keep house. Second, my father was also unemployed at this time. He was studying.

The roots of both my paternal and maternal ancestors go way back to the very origins of the Zlatoust factories—more than two hundred years—and all of them were workers, although a few of them were masters. For example, my maternal grandfather was so decorated for his skills that he was given his salary—this was in the days of the czar, of course—in gold ten-ruble coins.

My father was wonderfully talented and this was evident in literally everything he did. From him I inherited my memory, my intuition for creative solutions in difficult situations, and my love for stability, precision, and harmony. But in my father these qualities manifested themselves more clearly than with me. For example, when Larisa was a student at the polytechnic institute, she noted that, when my father was helping her with her homework on USSR state standard specifications, he never once consulted the manuals. It turns out he remembered them all—tens of thousands of them—and never made a mistake.

As an organizer he was brilliant. No matter what phase of production he was sent to, he quickly got to know the people, their strengths and goals, and put them in conditions where they could work with maximum satisfaction and output.

I also feel this organizing vein in myself, but I'm more trusting in my judgment of people and more linear in the ways I work with them. As a result, I've been disillusioned and mistaken about people, which, if memory serves me, never happened with my father.

Nonetheless, he is a guide for me in dealing with people. When I participate in solving my country's social problems, I turn to my memories of him in difficult moments and think, How would my father act here?, and I can discover the solution.

He had no special schooling in his youth, but he still made a career for himself. His talent was spotted immediately. Whatever he applied himself to, it came out better and brighter than it did for others. It's not surprising that whenever a vacancy opened up, my father was nominated for it right away. He didn't remain a mere worker for long. He was appointed in rapid succession to foreman, shift engineer, and, finally, senior shift engineer.

But that's as far as it went. The next step, shop manager, was out of reach. The shop in itself was a large enterprise, a factory within a factory. My father knew manufacturing and could manage people. Had he become shop manager he would have "fulfilled the plan" no less competently than his predecessors, but he saw this position differently. In his mind the shop manager was the helmsman. He had to look at the whole picture, to imagine it not just tomorrow but the day after tomorrow. He had to view its development not only in the context of the factory, but of the whole industry. In short, he had to be up on new materials and new technologies. In order to grow further and not let his career slide or wind up in a dead-end position, he needed a piece of paper, a technical education diploma. I don't consider higher education obligatory for talented people. With my father it was not so much a case of knowledge and skills as it was the formal right to take upon himself more responsibility.

Father studied three years in Moscow at the Bauman Higher Technical School. This was a specialized course that turned experienced workers into certified specialists. When I remember the want, even destitution, in which we lived, it is those three years that come most to mind. We didn't live so well prior to them, either, but were like everyone else around us. Thank God we didn't live in poverty. Eventually, Father received a raise and our life started to get better.

However, those three years cannot be dismissed. Father got a stipend of 700 rubles from the factory. Converted to the present exchange rate, the highest you come up with is 140 rubles (about $225.00 at the official rate of exchange), and barely that. Half he kept for himself, and half he left us. Even to make ends meet on this small amount for three people was out of the question, so Mama earned money by sewing at night. She sewed well, but her clientele was the same—our circle. The work was priced cheaply not because people didn't want to pay more but because they couldn't! Like us, they had trouble making ends meet, and to pay a tailor meant to deprive themselves of something else.

No matter how small these fees were, at least we had them, and we survived on them for three long years, although it subsequently came out that Mama didn't get off so easily: her eyesight drastically weakened. I found out about this much later. To say that I am sorry for Mama's misfortune is the same as saying nothing. Still, no matter how bitter Mama's loss, I can only think about those evenings with tenderness. And how many there were! Engraved by time, warmed by emotional proximity, preserved in the heart . . . Larisa is already sleeping, for she has to get up early for school; the cat is rolled up in a ball at my side, and I am only pretending to sleep. I see through the bars of my bed how Mama is bent over her sewing. I hear how she quietly hums and how her Singer softly patters from time to time. I know precisely how long it is until Father returns, but still I ask, "Mom, how many days left until Papa comes?" "We counted them today. Fifty-two. Now go to sleep, the time will go faster, and the days will be less." "No," I say, "tomorrow will also be fifty-two, because we didn't count today."

I wished the time would pass more quickly. Had it been possible, I probably would have refused those days without Father. Even if they were jam-packed, without Father the most important part was missing, and therefore I wouldn't have been sorry at all to lose them.

My closeness to this person, the feeling of inseparability from him and the feeling of continuity with him, was incredible. I felt almost physically how my life had grown from his and, when he wasn't around, it was not as if I were left without roots or soil. It simply meant a drought, and I had to learn patience, somehow had to hold out until the day his face would appear in the frame of the sooty train window, and I would burst from Mama's embrace and run alongside the window on the platform, bumping into people and shouting something from excitement, and he would stand, pressed to the glass, looking at me. And then he would exit from the car and put his things on the platform, and I would leap into his arms and whisper, "Papa, Papochka."

*   *   *

When did chess first appear in my life? It seems to me that it was always there, a part of my childhood, inseparable from my father. Chess was an important part of his world, always available to me even when he wasn't. Chess gave me the feeling that any minute he would walk through the door, see me playing with the pieces, and smile, saying, "Play, son, play. That's always a good thing. Just don't forget afterward to count the pieces and put them back. There must be order in everything." Yet order is the one thing he couldn't instill in me. Perhaps it's because we saw each other so infrequently, or perhaps there was something lacking in me.

At first the chessmen were simply toys with which I acted out scenes. But by the time I was four years old the game became more like military scenarios. I don't think there is a boy anywhere, if he has a chess set in his house, who hasn't done this. Chess, after all, is a school of war, hierarchy, and organization.

How pleasant it is not just to participate in, but to be the creator of, a whole world with its own laws, to be subordinate to it, and at the same time to reshape it with a free and powerful hand. Lying in bed for hours at a time, amid a complex landscape fashioned from the folds of the bedding, I carried out maneuvers and set ambushes. The scouts tried to penetrate the enemy camp, and woe to them if they were discovered; the cavalry easily overtook and trampled them to death. Then the brave officers took up reconnaissance, accompanied by their loyal soldiers who, if need be, could conceal the commander and let him get back to his own lines. Afterward the officers, having already returned to the head of major detachments, walked straight into the cannons, in closed formation, in defiance of the enemy's cavalry.

It's amazing what a great number of hours were spent at this game, but I never regretted them. Although I played at this chess warfare at age ten and even at eleven, an age when I did not simply play chess but was already a candidate for master and had four years' experience with the Chelyabinsk regional team, I don't consider them lost hours because this game was a constant, inexhaustible source of amusement, especially after the normal unpleasantries of childhood, as well as during my many periods of illness.

It was from this childish game that the player in me was born. It was here that I came to understand chess and its laws, as well as develop a feel for its elements and forces. It was here that I developed an ability to blend with, and inhabit, the game naturally and freely. To be sure, all this matured at a later date as I continued to learn new games whose basic laws (it's clear, I hope, that I'm not speaking about rules) I discovered and formulated for myself, but it had its roots in childhood. I remember how the principles of that game changed and how it became my first proving ground.

Still I knew that, besides my game with the chess pieces, there existed another game with these same pieces on a checkered board, a game adults enjoyed playing, an incomprehensible and mysterious game that was therefore all the more alluring to me.

I came to know it as a spectator, and nothing more. My parents were convinced that an early contact with chess would be too great a burden for my childish mind.

They said no, and I didn't argue. In our house it wasn't customary to say something twice. So I watched.

Chess meant my father. I observed the game only on those rare occasions when he was on leave from Moscow, when one of his friends would come by and they would play for long hours into the evening, sometimes past midnight.

My place was on my father's knees. We had an agreement: I could sit and watch, but I could not disturb him. I sat quietly. This was difficult, but I tried. I was glad of any conversation, for then I could say something, obviously having nothing to do with position or game plan—because I still didn't understand any of this—but I would say the first words that came into my head. When they laughed, I laughed, too, and louder. When they got distracted in some conversation away from the game, I seized the chance to carry out on the table a common military skirmish, but only with those pieces already removed from the board.

Now the conversation between my father and his friend had finished and in the same instant, in midflight and midblow, my battle died down. An agreement is an agreement. Besides, I realized that the action on the chessboard is incomparably more interesting than the encounters among the pieces on the table. The reasons are many. I felt the harmony of the game, the way in which the pawns and pieces move about. Their invisible cohesion, hitherto incomprehensible to me, became perfectly real. Sometimes, though, the impression of harmony vanished. I still didn't understand why this was so, but I sensed that something was not quite right. From the tension in Father's knees, on which I was sitting, or from the withdrawal of his hands embracing me, I realized that he too had seen something wrong and didn't like his position. He had experience, so it's understandable, but how did I know something was wrong?

I liked the game's fairness, which doesn't give preference to anyone. Time and time again I convinced myself that the player whose harmony is preserved longer will win. It is not the number of pawns and pieces, but harmony, focusing all the energy of the remaining soldiers, that determines who will come out ahead. It is harmony that takes the upper hand, even against a numerically superior opponent.

I liked the goodness of this game. To the very last moment, to the very last move, it gives even a hopelessly lost player a chance. The player who sticks with it to the end can always count upon a happy outcome. I understand this.

Gradually, I began discovering the rules of the game by myself. If you observe chess games evening after evening, this will take place naturally. At some point I began to understand the technical execution of almost every move. (However, I couldn't grasp two things on my own: castling and the capture of pawns *en passant*. Father had to explain them to me.) But the ultimate meaning of these moves in a game was still far from clear.

Then, like an image in a photographic print, the principles of battle began to show through, and here things got easier. I already had great experience with chess warfare in bed and this, combined with the criterion of harmony, helped me understand the meaning of each move.

This is how I saw it. Pawns not only create the sketch for the whole painting, they are also the soil, the foundation, of any position. They are leaned on, hidden behind, and used to overcome any obstacle. It is extremely important to observe how currents run through the pawn formations and how energy collects in those places where the pawns, like little islands, wedge their way into the position of the enemy and stand to the death. Even if the pawns are torn asunder, this is irrelevant. The main thing is that they do not violate the inner harmony of the position, and that they be linked by a common idea and those same invisible currents.

The officers (for a long time I couldn't understand why adults called them *bishops*), like machine gunners, have to occupy key positions and support the infantry from there. If a machine gunner reaches the enemy camp, then you can be sure that right there is the weakest spot in the defense.

The cavalry has to lie in ambush, intimidating not so much by its strength as by its unpredictability. More often than not, its attacks are merely demonstrations, but you have to be on your guard and not let the moment pass when it is time to trumpet their retreat. For the enemy there is no greater satisfaction than to entice your cavalry into a trap and fire at it point-blank.

The Turks (rooks) seemed to me dense and conceitedly linear, and their excessive strength saved them from any need for fantasy. If you have strength, you don't need intellect. They rested their hopes upon their mass, just like the boys in our courtyard who were all significantly older and bigger than I and who, consequently, never considered me for any of their activities. Since everything about the Turks was already known, I didn't like them but merely tolerated them, and then only with the condition that they not abuse their clumsiness. Sometimes, however, they were rolled out onto the very front ranks in direct sight of the enemy, and then I expressed both sympathy and interest toward them.

In my bed warfare there was no place for queens. They were helpless and easily vulnerable in battle, and it was beyond their powers to make any movement along the quagmire of the bedding's nap. Thus, I didn't seek out a role for them. But in the game I observed from my father's knees, I couldn't fail to hold in high regard their striking ability to organize the chess plane around themselves, as well as the colossal energy with which they could enliven any position. Ultimately, I felt their possibilities were great because they embodied perfection. Still, their elitism bothered me. I felt they were of a different world, not of mine, that they were cut from a different cloth.

During my game of chess war I imagined that I was the pawns. I was impressed by their selflessness and readiness for self-sacrifice. In their small stature I recognized myself. I affirmed myself and my strengthening character in their steadfastness and stubbornness. When I led the officers into battle, I did so with a detached glance; never did I have the desire to become one of them.

The luxury, impressiveness, and regal strength of the queens made me look up to them against my will, but I couldn't reconcile myself to this. Giving them their due, I nonetheless rejoiced when I saw that it was beyond them to breach a friendly pawn formation, and I celebrated when a pawn struck a deadly blow to this Athena of the chessboard. In moments such as these I didn't regret that harmony which fell by the wayside. It was as if I knew that a real queen would never allow herself to perish in the beginning of a game, or even in the middle. She recognizes both her responsibility as protectress of harmony and her function of cementing a position. If she is to perish, then in so doing she must deal the enemy a lethal blow.

Finally, the king ... For a long time I understood him to be the goal, the prize. This notion was directly transplanted from my bed wars onto the chessboard. It suited me while I merely played chess, and even when I became a grand master. But in preparing for a match against Robert Fischer, comparing his vision of chess with mine, and having the opportunity not just to interpret concrete chess positions—which, incidentally, is how a chess professional spends the greater part of his time—but to reflect awhile on chess as a system of values, I understood why, subconsciously, the figure of the king was ultimately dissatisfying to me. To simply be a prize is trivial for him, and to be a victim is just downright stupid. The king is endowed not just with exclusive powers, but with exclusive possibilities. There isn't another fighter like him. If he is a queen in miniature, he is also perfection, and perfection always possesses vast energy. Consequently, perfection always serves as organizer of the board. Thus I arrived at the idea of a bipole in the organization of my chess position. When there were poles in a position—not only queen, but king as well— the position took on new cohesion and new energy, meaning that its completeness (nearness to perfection and ability to perfect itself) became significantly greater.

As to how I went from a chess spectator to a participant, there is an amusing story in our family.

My parents feared chess might become an excessive burden on my childish mind. But it was impossible to learn how the pieces move, to be a player by calling and not play chess. So I began to play by myself. At first it was the occasional imaginary war, which was enough to satisfy me completely. Yet there was something enigmatic about the game that I still could not grasp. Gradually I drew myself into it. I set out the pieces and took turns making moves, first White, then Black, just like my father and his friends.

I suspect that, for the first few dozen times, these games were a reenactment of my bed war, except here, instead of the bedding, the chessmen moved along the black and white squares according to the rules. True, I had to make slight corrections in the unusual strategy. Pawns, for example, don't move backwards, a principle that instilled in me responsibility for each attack by my loyal soldiers. Still, the basic plan and action remained the same and, therefore, any contact of hostile figures ended in bloodshed. The battlefield emptied with frightening rapidity. When there remained just a few fighters on each side, I took stock of the situation, stopped, and began to think.

I had to understand how a fair number of fighters could be preserved on one side, while at the same time the other side had half as many. Did this mean I had done something wrong until then? I recalled the sequence of my actions, move by move. Since my memory allowed it, everything was imprinted with photographic precision. Analysis, however, did not yield results, and I could not grasp the essence of my mistakes. This had to be the reason, or otherwise how else can one explain why the next struggle on the board began with the same violent carnage?

At this juncture, though, the game did not end. Each side still had forces, albeit unequal, and my sense of fairness naturally inclined me to sympathize with the weaker of the two. It was difficult to become reconciled with this sympathy. Giveaways offended me. And then I discovered the meaning and cost of space on the chessboard. Only space allowed for maneuvering, the creation of threats without coming into direct contact, and distraction with a false move so that suddenly, altering direction, you could deliver a real blow.

Naturally this was not recognized immediately. Experience accumulated bit by bit, eventually becoming knowledge. This was not just formulated knowledge, but something within me, because the next time I made use of it automatically.

This self-education in chess did not last long. At first Mama did not attach any significance to my games on the board, especially since they rarely took place, but one day she noticed that I was spending an inordinate amount of time at it. She took a long, hard look and realized that I was not simply having fun nor imitating the game, trying to act like an adult. She realized that I was actually playing. How close this activity was to real chess she didn't wait to find out. Remembering the danger about my mind, she firmly removed the board and that was that—or so she thought.

The poison of chess had already entered into my bloodstream. The sweetness of forbidden fruit is widely known. I had become addicted to chess and didn't have the slightest desire to refuse this drug. I didn't have to look for an outlet—it revealed itself naturally: I began to play in my mind. As it turned out, this did not pose any difficulty for me. I mentally saw the board as well as the pieces, which obediently executed any movement I could think up. Since this didn't require the slightest effort on my part, I didn't see anything special about it. I had no doubt that every chess player, and especially an adult chess player, could play in his head.

Somehow my discovery coincided with illness, a common condition for me. As I was not permitted to crawl out from under the covers, my ability to carry out military action was highly restricted. Instead of the vast expanses of the bed, on which nothing limited my fantasy, I was only able to make use of a small patch. I moved closer to the wall and lay on my side so that the playing territory became larger, but this was still not enough. I was deprived of maneuverability, which inevitably led to swift battles. Due to their frequent repetition, their attraction was sharply devalued, and the dynamics, deprived of thought, could not break the boredom.

Chess came to the rescue. Suddenly it turned out that I could play as many times in a row as I wanted and not be bored with it. This was an astounding revelation. Only now am I putting into words that feeling which overcame me then: the feeling of a seafarer, certain he has discovered a small island and suddenly realizing that, in fact, it's the edge of a gigantic land mass. But back then I simply rejoiced that I could find pleasure in the process of playing the game over and over, varying the plans and destroying them with a countergame, or being crafty with myself by giving the weaker side more of my energy.

When a child is ill and has nothing to keep him busy, he usually sulks and demands attention or languishes in a state of semidrowsiness. Here Mama noticed that her son was behaving somewhat strangely. I didn't sleep or play with toys, but simply lay with a faraway look on my face. Everything would have been fine, but suddenly she remembered that perhaps half an hour or maybe more than an hour had passed since she had seen me like this. Mama became alarmed and called to me, but I just waved her away. Coming nearer, she sensed a tension within me. Her child was thinking! This should have been cause for joy, but she didn't know what to make of it. She stood there, looking at me, and then suddenly it dawned on her. "Are you playing chess?"

I nodded and again waved her away. "Stop it this instant!" I stopped, but when Mama left, I turned to the wall to make her think I was sleeping, re-created in my memory the position of the interrupted game, and, as if nothing had happened, continued to play.

To my parents' credit it should be said that they understood the situation and futility of any ban. However, the situation did have to be brought under control. That same evening Father pulled up a chair alongside my bed with the chessboard in hand, arranged the pieces on it, and said, "Well, son, show me what you can do." It was late autumn. I was only four years old.

I was so excited by the very fact of playing Father—the realization of a distant dream—that I conducted the first game practically in a delirium. I hurried. I hastened to show what I knew. I wanted to surprise Father by showing him that I was capable of everything. I grabbed first at one piece and then another, not because I was full of plans but full of excitement. Then I suddenly came to and saw that my army was almost entirely decimated and I couldn't remember when and how it disappeared. Father's army had barely suffered any casualties at all, while steadily advancing and occupying, so it seemed to me, the whole board. This was a horrible rout. Moreover, as I understand it now, Father was barely involved

in the game. He only made sure that his pieces domi-
nated and controlled the board, and that they didn't fall
in the path of my blind moves.

Father didn't pay attention to this, or carry the game
out to checkmate, or even concern himself with the
results. He diplomatically offered me a compromise. "We
don't have too many pieces left, there's hardly anything
left to play with . . ."

"But didn't you see, Papa, how my pieces fought?"

"They fought temperamentally and fearlessly. Only I
don't understand what their commander wanted. Let's
do it again from the beginning, but this time, son, don't
hurry."

It turned out that the sense of that very first game was
in the game itself, in the process, in self-expression and
contact with my father. The result, as a fixation of the
correlation of forces, yielded to an emotional evaluation.
Who would have thought that this would stay with me
forever? This first game was a lesson in graciousness, a
lesson in understanding. (Later, as world champion, I
would try not to beat the youngest players but offer them
instead a draw.) Even though the purpose of the game
is to win, its higher meaning lies in self-expression,
acquiring inner freedom.

At the same time my father provided me with the key
for removing the main contradiction in our little affair.
A player (and I was already then a player, although I
didn't realize it until ten years later) has to win. This is
why he plays. However, it is not an irrepressible thirst
to win that draws him to the game but the game itself,
its process. The game reconciles him to life, with all its
routine, confusion, and tedium, and to the inevitable
defeat in the end. This means the game is not a flight

from reality, not *playing* at life, nor even its surrogate. Everything is contained within it, including immortality.

Again we set up the pieces and I, almost as soon as I lightly touched the pawn at e2 (I still didn't know that the game could be commenced with other moves), immediately forgot Father's instructions and desperately plunged ahead. This time, though, Father wouldn't allow it. To his way of thinking, the basis of any undertaking, including chess, is order.

"Don't hurry," he said. "Think first, and then move."

The most elementary precept, or so it would seem. I understood it right away, both its meaning and truth, but I couldn't do it. Some kind of demon sat in me, and hardly had my turn come than it pushed my hand to make an immediate response. In short, during this evening I showed that I was capable of very little. I knew how to move, how to strike, and how to construct the most primitive plans. But to take into account someone else's thinking, someone else's will, or imagine someone else's plan—this so far was beyond the bounds of my horizon.

It would be so tempting to describe the impetuous formation of the wunderkind; show how he apprehends everything in midsentence, at the first hint; how yesterday's clumsy little lad metamorphoses into an invincible chess warrior, a player for whom all the unwritten rules of the game are revealed.

Alas, the truth is much more prosaic. The truth is that my chess development was nothing out of the ordinary, and it proceeded probably at a pace no faster than others. Judge for yourself: I needed almost three years to catch up to Father and play with him as an equal. A whole three years! He was not a particularly strong player, either. At his best he played at the level of a second-category player. A strong amateur, but that's it. True, we weren't equals for long. Already by my eighth birthday I was regularly coming out on top, and by age nine we quit our chess duels altogether as they were becoming totally devoid of interest.

It would seem there is a contradiction here. On the one hand, I maintain that my chess development progressed at an ordinary pace; on the other, it did not stop at the second or first ranking, as with the overwhelming majority of strong amateurs. In childhood I surpassed all my contemporaries, then adults, and rather assuredly and swiftly I ascended to the chess throne. Why? What contributed to my overcoming the barrier of mediocrity which stops almost all others?

When I state that my chess development proceeded at a normal pace it means that, in order to raise myself up to each successive step along the way to becoming a chess master, I had to play a definite number of games. For some this is a greater number, for others less, but in general a certain range exists. Thus, if my friends in the courtyard played their first thousand games, say, over a period of three years, I accomplished the same feat in roughly six months (although, in reality, I think I needed a significantly shorter period). I played with myself, with Father, and with my friends. They loved to watch, but I played. I did everything possible to be a participant, not a spectator. Precisely because of this improbable tempo I was able to compress time considerably. This in itself was enough for others to sense the presence of a wunderkind in their midst.

However, there were two small engines that powered my boat. My friends played for pleasure, and so did I. They found satisfaction in the process of the game, and so did I. But if for them everything began and ended with pleasure, then for me, as for any genuine player, pleasure was indistinct from victory. When they lost, it was a loss and nothing more, but for me, any loss was a failure which should not have happened; if it did, it meant that somewhere I had made a mistake which I had to make sure wouldn't happen again.

There was not enough emotion in the process of the game to satisfy me. I had to win, and win all the time. To do so, I had to find an algorithm to success, my combination of "three-seven-ace" which no one could withstand. If my friends thought about chess only in the process of the game itself, at the board, then I lived and breathed chess. Chess was always with me.

My playing took on a new quality, not so much as a consequence of statistical processes as it was the result of single-minded work. Second, the energy which I put into each game, to say nothing of separate and key moves, gave rise to a compact style of playing uncommon for my contemporaries. The third point is that, at first unconsciously and then more consciously, I sought harmony on the chessboard. I still didn't understand the secret of this harmony, but its fruits—an indestructible vitality and victoriousness—were obvious to me.

As any players knows, the path of least resistance never leads to victory, certainly not to great victory. To survive, to hold out, to keep the balance, while hoping that luck doesn't fluctuate, is the maximum that someone swimming with the current can count on in a game. What is at the basis of this philosophy? Advantage. This is the tune he dances to, this is his true goal. A player, however, has a completely different philosophy, and therefore a different goal. A player plays in order *to live through an adventure*. In playing, he *overcomes*—overcomes himself, circumstances, and fate.

A player would never go to such expense just for the sake of advantage. Advantage, in of itself, is boring to him. It is desirable, as it would be for any normal person, but boring. And since a genuine player seeks experiences, any form of boredom, including boredom for the sake of advantage, is counterproductive. Thus, when he feels that boredom is at hand, he drives it away instantly by a simple method: he raises the stakes, regardless of the cards he's holding at the time.

But for now I am tiny and weak, sitting on my knees in a chair. Before me, in a corner of the table, is a chessboard, and across from me is Father. He is leaning back slightly in his chair, making his face seem sunburned in the shade from the fringe of the lampshade hovering above us. On the board his latest rout of me is in full swing. It is already too late to regroup, either by cleverness or force, the remainder of my army, scattered along the margins.

"In two moves you'll be checkmated," says Father.

I see this. I already know enough about chess that, in addition to my own moves, I can predict Father's. Usually just one or two moves ahead, but sometimes, in following the obvious logic of one of his abrupt moves, I can guess the whole series, and this thrills me beyond belief.

I see that in two moves I'll be mated. I see there's no salvation, and I begin to cry. I don't do this completely on purpose, for I already know that I will feel better once the tears dry, but I can also move my father to pity. In the next game he'll either surrender or else play in such a way that it ends in a truce, with both armies completely destroyed. I know ahead of time the tender expression of his face and eyes, the words of comfort, and the touch of his hand stroking my hair. This time, though, there is to be none of that. Father's eyes are so cold and hard.

"Listen, son," he says, in an emphatically clear voice, "remember this. If you start bawling one more time, I'll never play with you again."

In our house it wasn't customary to say something twice. My tears dried up. This is how I came to know one of the most important rules of the game: Threat is more terrible than execution.

Before the tale about chess leads me out of childhood, I want to say a few words about my health. So much has been written about it in connection with my successes and failures that it's probably not a bad idea if my views on this subject were to become known.

Mama says that I was born healthy. In any case, in the first months of life there weren't any serious problems. But then I fell ill with whooping cough, and in its most serious form. My condition deteriorated before everyone's eyes. I lost consciousness, choked, and ran at the mouth. As usual, medicine was useless, and the pediatrician (I remember well this nice woman, since she was the only physician I knew in childhood) told this to Mama. I can't imagine what words can be used to inform a mother that her son is dying, but she somehow said them.

At that time both my maternal and paternal grandmothers were still alive. They were pious and resolute women. What's this—bury an unchristened child? They insisted that the christening take place immediately.

The month was November. Snow fell during the night. The matins had ended long ago, the church had cooled off, and it was brisk inside. As witnesses said later, "You could almost see your breath." You can imagine what the water in the font was like.

My grandmothers knew the priest and explained the situation to him. Fortunately, he turned out to be experienced in such matters. "I'll do everything that's proper," he said. "After that, the Lord will judge him." And he dunked me in the font headfirst, holding me under the water to stop my breathing artificially.

The stress worked gloriously. I shouted for the whole church to hear, the priest burst out laughing and cried, "He will live!" Swear to God, foaming and coughing ceased abruptly, and in several days my health improved. Now there's a miraculous recovery.

Nevertheless, the sickness had taken its toll. My nasopharynx has remained weak my whole life. Colds, flu, pharyngitis, rhinitis, you name it, were my days, my norm. I got so accustomed to them that I virtually stopped noticing their presence, nor for that matter did I consider them to be a hindrance to my chess activities.

This continued right up until my thirtieth year.

I have heard that, for each person who leads an intense life and fails to pay attention to his health, there is a certain boundary. Up to that boundary one's body functions, as it were, normally, but once beyond it, the body suddenly begins to break down. For men the fatal line is usually considered to be age forty. I managed to cross it ten years earlier.

Perhaps I am being somewhat dramatic. It's possible that this was only the first warning bell, because the breaking point had not yet been reached. My body still had room to withdraw. When fatigue, accumulated over a long period from the struggle with colds, seriously upset my equilibrium, it was as if a kind of governor switched itself on, and my body shifted downward to another, more economical regime.

I didn't notice it right away, because it still wasn't reflected in my successes; as before, I was winning the major tournaments. But the price of each victory shot up precipitously. What I had once accomplished with ease now cost me incredible effort. It felt as if my brain were clogged with wadding. To get it to work, I had to concentrate all my will, but in so doing I only made the situation worse by expending more energy than I had. A kind of emptiness within surfaced more often, and more often I had to ask myself: How can I play if there is no strength to concentrate, no strength to hold my attention on an important point?

Against my will, I had to save myself with stereotypes, standard solutions, which always caused me boredom, and which I avoided with all conceivable means, sometimes at great and imprudent risk. Risk, however, demands vigilance and a keen intellect.

In short, my body could not handle the dual load of fighting against illness while guaranteeing a sufficiently high intellectual level. Youth had passed. I still considered myself young, but something had truly gone with the years. It wasn't courage, but boldness. I began to experience it on extremely rare occasions, and I felt this loss of boldness as practically the most serious deficit at that time.

And then one day I matured. I realized, with unusual clarity, that if I still wanted to play chess at the highest level, I had to improve my health. This meant repudiating the most common clichés, such as health comes from God; if it's there, it's there, and if not, then go with what you have.

I didn't put faith in medicine and, besides, medicine wasn't interested in me. Doctors want a real disease, something they can read in a tomograph or at least in an X ray, or something that can be excised or suppressed with drugs. I dangled somewhere in the border zone between health and sickness. I felt I was waning, but the doctors only shrugged their shoulders: others live with it and get by.

There remained sports. For example, tennis, which I had tried long ago, and swimming, skiing in the winter and running in summer.

I attempted it once and quit (so many things to do in a day, and each one more important than training), tried it a second time and again it wouldn't go. Moreover, my first attempts were met with skepticism among my close friends. In their perception of me, I was inseparable from sickliness and disease. Some of them even went to extremes, saying that I was able to beat everyone in my powerless and virtually transparent condition. Therefore, their line of reasoning continued, it's not a question of health, but something else which I'd lost. Go back and find what was lost, and everything will be the same as before.

Can you imagine? I listened to all this nonsense and found meaning in it. What ruses you allow yourself at times just to avoid doing something.

The path of least resistance is so attractive! Yet I knew

that it leads downward to nowhere. So many wrecks and broken fates I had seen among those who succumbed to it. Once there, there's no turning back. So what then: Give in to cowardice and then, for the rest of my life, think that here was the moment when I still had a chance to turn off, when I still had a chance to test fate once again, and I didn't make the best of it? Intuition told me that I hadn't developed my resources or potential to their utmost. Far from it!

I lost almost two years to this vacillating back and forth. Besides the time, I lost the title of world champion. This was the second bell. I understood that the third might be the final one, and right then and there I took matters into my own hands. Gradually and quietly, but regularly, one day at a time. Whereas the alternative path led downward, this one led into the unknown, but I already knew that I would follow it to the end. Thank God I still had some character.

My body responded literally to the very first timid attempts to help it. It hardly knew me already! In order to counterbalance the temptation of laziness, it rushed to meet me in bursts of an unusual and excellent physical condition.

I didn't have to torture myself or suffer, as all modern coaches demand. Nor did I have to muddle through exhausting cross-country races in the sands of the Caspian beaches under a scorching sun, as Gary Kasparov does. No matter what I did, be it tennis, running, swimming, or gymnastics, I found that tempo and sense of rhythm which was right for me, and it worked.

Right then, for the first time, I thought: I've always believed that I have taken from life absolutely everything it has allotted me, but here it turns out that what was allotted was incomparably more. There's no point in fretting over it, but it mustn't be forgotten. It could have been a completely different life and a different fate.

For the first time in my life I had the prospect of harmony of body and soul, not on that miserable level which my body permitted me, but on a level which was instilled in my nature.

I don't pretend to anything more than harmony.

Harmony presupposes such a condition of the body in which it not only ceases to be a cause for failure, but generally ceases to be an object of attention. It's as if the body is nonexistent, and a person freely raises himself to the level of his spiritual desires.

I want to clarify something right away. I do not have perfection in mind, at least for the reason that I have always valued very modestly what nature has given me. To others whom it gave more, let them worry about it. Perhaps knowledge of the limitations of my possibilities also explains why I thought very rarely about such lofty matters. Simply put, I am a pragmatic and practical person by nature. Life makes me that way! If I do think about such things, then it's only in connection with chess. Back then, though, these thoughts didn't assume any concrete, general character. After all, a chess game is not created by one person, but two, and not in collaboration, but in combat and counteraction, in destroying the plans of one's opponent. How can one speak of perfection via destruction?

Yet perfection, or something close to perfection, does sometimes appear on the chessboard. Where does it come from? It is the creative idea that brings it to life. In any beautiful chess game there undoubtedly exists a creative idea and, as practice shows, the more truthful such an idea, the more energy is contained within it and the more invincible it becomes. Here the combination and mutual enrichment of two opposing creative ideas leads to chess perfection.

I must reiterate that during a match you usually don't think about this. Maybe that's wrong. As a rule, the one who loses is usually the one who errs last. Great opportunities for victory, even in the wake of technical omissions, belong to those whose creative ideas are more fecund and more accurately reveal the essense of a key position.

Now, a few years after I began the task of restoring my health, I can say that I have lost the sense of age. I feel better now than I did when I was twenty, and I am capable of much more. My body stopped being a drag on me; now I boldly rely upon it, and it almost never lets me down. It is prepared to pull any load my soul can harness. I have returned to the highest levels of chess. Everything will be fine as long as my soul doesn't let me down. Sometimes I catch myself for not having the same interest in this fight as before. It's already been played, and more than once. I've tried everything and know everything. What can I say—sometimes it just gets boring. Perhaps what I really need to do is strive for a higher register, something higher than concrete games or concrete matches, higher than the battle with Kasparov, and think more about perfection. That's something I surely can't get bored with! But how can I recognize that reasonable limitation to which I pretend? How can I reconcile my possibilities with my dream? Or is a dream the measure of our true possibilities?

*   *   *

Anyway, it's time to finish with illnesses so that we don't have to return to them any more in this book.

Though I was sick often (you might even say that it was a normal condition for me to be sick), I never had to go to the hospital. My whole life I have been in the hospital only twice, once for a concussion of the brain (I slipped in winter on an icy stone) and once for diphtheria. I almost had to go a third time when doctors discovered I had rheumatic heart disease at the age of seven. They threw such a scare into my parents that they took me straightaway to the hospital. To my delight, the place was quarantined because of some infection, and the other wards were filled beyond capacity. I wasn't refused admission, but advised to wait a bit. My parents' excitement died down, too, during the drive to the hospital and after being hassled in the various wards. They decided to put the whole thing off for another week or two, and then until summer so as not to interfere with my schooling, and then finally they concluded that perhaps it would just go away by itself. And, in fact, it did go away. To this day, I still don't know exactly—knock on wood—where my heart is, but Mama and I remember this incident every time doctors frighten someone among our close friends with terrible diseases. We're not calling the competence of the doctors into doubt, but it's indisputable that some of them, in enhancing their reputations, love to conjure up ghosts.

I liked being sick at home.

As to why this is so, it's difficult to say, even now. During school years, of course, it's easy to explain: You don't have to get up early and you don't have to sit in class. Even before school, though, staying in bed didn't produce any negative emotions in me. The chance to play chess and war was not enhanced because it wasn't directly tied to health. Maybe it was the contact with Mama. The "quantity time" didn't change, but the "quality time" definitely did. This by no means implies that I was lacking in maternal tenderness. Mama was generous with that in her relationship with me, as were my sister and father. In general, I have the feeling from those years that everyone loved me. There's never too much tenderness and I, like an experienced hunter or sensitive dial, responded to its slightest change.

Mama, of course, diligently took care of me. Her actions were honed to the point of being automatic. I became so used to all these compresses, pills, mixtures, mustard plasters, and jars that I didn't react to them on an emotional level at all. The only thing I categorically wouldn't do was try to cure myself by sweating the disease out—the traditional Russian method. My father considered it to be the panacea for all ailments and it was the only cure he ever used.

For just such an occasion Mama always kept an emergency jar of raspberry jam and a bottle of Cahors wine. When my father wasn't feeling well and complained of a stomachache, Mama, with an eye to the night ahead, brewed strong tea, dissolved the jam in it, and then mixed it half-and-half with hot Cahors wine. Father drank it down and then climbed under the covers so that only his eyes and nose were sticking out. And he sweated. He sweated so much that you could wring the sheets out. To endure this torture and not make even the slightest little hole in the covers demanded the strongest possible character and heart. My father had that. In the morning, as if nothing at all had happened, he went off to work completely sound.

I took after Mama. The only thing that neither of us can brag about having is patience. Even the greatest love for Father and a willingness to be like him in everything could not make me endure this torment to the end. Not once.

CHAPTER TWO

THE FIRST CHESS TERRITORY I conquered was our courtyard. Procedures here were much more democratic than the strictness of my father's chess. There was a courtyard hierarchy, but it was outweighed by the fraternity of people with a common love for chess.

I didn't have to ask for a place near the table—it was offered to me. Usually one of the older kids just picked me up so I could watch the game in comfort. I didn't have to beg these people to bring me into the game. All I had to do was wait my turn, and take the place of the loser and show everyone what I could do. Even if I lost in three moves or played everyone in a row, what mattered was that my fate was in my own hands.

I didn't join in the game right away, because I didn't want to lose. I took losing badly with my father, but a loss to him wasn't shameful. In our chess crowd, though, the young boys were twice my age. As far as the adults there were concerned, I was under foot.

Chess, in addition to everything else, is a great game because everyone is equal in its presence. Chess doesn't discriminate. When we all got to know each other, all these big kids and adults became "Uncle Vanya," "Uncle Petya," "Kolya," "Mitya," and so on. The age difference became irrelevant—what mattered was how one played.

On the porch or under a birch tree, five or six members would gather. There couldn't have been more than about fifteen people in our club. Realizing that I could contend with some of them, one day I took a chance and jumped out of turn. Though I figured no one would mock me, it was still a surprise to hear their encouragement: "Our troops have arrived!" and "Way to go, Tolik, it's about time!"

Not long before this I had turned six. I was still very anxious, but less so than in my first game with Father. I was already experienced from playing dozens of games at home, and I knew how each of the courtyard chess players played his game. And at least here, a loss wasn't considered a dishonor. The opponent I drew, Sasha Kolyshkin—a future friend—was by no means one of the strongest players. Five years older than I, he was in the same class as Larisa and until that day he had probably never noticed me.

So that I could see the board, a wooden crate was placed on my bench. How distant this sultry Sunday was from my first game with Father. Then I was happy at the very opportunity to play. This feeling still remained, but now it served as background and shading. The subject of the drawing had changed. I was a player and I entered the game to win. I had advantages, and I knew it.

First of all, Sasha Kolyshkin naturally didn't take me seriously, meaning that I could calculate the first dozen moves, and even more, from his carefree attitude to the game. Second, as I already knew his attacks, I had decided beforehand how to resist. My delight in playing depended upon how far Sasha would overdo things, and to what degree he would compromise his position. Third, when the real playing began (and I knew it would begin, for Sasha would never surrender to a little brat like me) I hoped that I would have the necessary skill and discipline to realize my goal. Everything turned out the way I thought it would.

But in the endgame, with a crushing advantage and excited by my audience, I began showing off. My moves were thoughtless and obvious. Finally, the harmony of the game disintegrated, but I was too busy hamming it up to notice. It wasn't the loss that surprised me—I had prepared myself for defeat—but the feeble way in which I lost. This was a shock. I could have won. My very first game in the courtyard, and I had prepared for it so much, and thought everything through, and I lost miserably.

You're waiting to hear that I burst out crying. After all, so young, and such a bitter disappointment. I won't lie. I won't describe my manly efforts to remember my father's advice. In fact, I didn't keep a stiff upper lip at all—I started bawling. I sat on the unsanded boards of my crate and cried. My older chess mates tried to console me, expressing amazement at the sudden turn of events in the game. I heard them, but I ignored them until someone grabbed me under the arm, lifted me up, and put me down on the ground. It seems the others had just as suddenly all forgotten about me, their backs turned toward the start of a new game. This, I understood, was the most important thing and, wiping away my tears, I asked in a breaking voice, "Who's last in line?"

*   *   *

A year later, when I was in the first grade, and late autumn had given way to a warm winter, I joined a chess club at the metal factory's Palace of Sport, the only place in town for chess. Inside were two large halls for basketball and weight lifting and a few smaller rooms for various other sports. The chess club was stuffed inside a tiny room crammed full with tables. Chess wasn't taught here—they didn't have the materials for that, or the teachers. People just played for hours at a time, dozens of games in a row.

My courtyard friends took me to the chess club. By this time each of them had managed to play in qualifying tournaments. At first they received the fifth ranking, then fourth—in those years the chess ladder was a long one. Then I learned that they were all signed up to play in a tournament for the third ranking. They were excited because the competition was so formidable and mere participation was an honor. So I began to think: Why shouldn't I try my hand? After all, I didn't play any worse than they did, and some of them were never able to beat me.

"Take me with you," I asked. They were amazed—each of them was older by five or six years and taller by at least a head. I was a baby to them, and it didn't matter that I was their equal in chess. My friends, amused by my request, took me with them the following evening. No one gave any thought to how it might turn out. Everything depended upon the leader, a Korean named Pak, and the breadth of his views, the level of his conservatism, and even his sense of humor. He would be seeing me for the first time, I was as small as could be, and a tournment for the third ranking, I emphasize, was a highly respectable event in our club.

"The kid plays as good as me," insisted Sasha Kolyshkin, failing to see the humor in his recommendation. "Karpov plays as good as me."

"Okay. I'll include your Karpov in the tournament. But first let him pass a test. He'll play a qualifying game with one of us. If he wins, he's in the tournament, but if he loses . . ."

Everyone agreed this was fair. Let them all see for themselves that they brought a real chess player, that I didn't need to be coddled. Pak looked around the room at all the old-timers of the club, and laughed. "Morkovin will play the qualifying game with Karpov."

This decision was met with enthusiasm. Morkovin was older than everyone (a year later we celebrated his seventy-fifth birthday), and there was something fitting about a meeting between the oldest and the youngest. The test Pak offered me only seemed serious—even if a person has played chess for more than fifty years, he's just not as quick in his seventies. No matter what Morkovin tried, I beat him. I took my rightful place in the tournament and played in it successfully, obtaining the third ranking in my very first attempt.

I studied chess at Mikhail Botvinnik's school, in its inaugural session. The school was founded in 1963 by the Trud sports society for its chess players. Conceived by Botvinnik, it was also run by him since there was no one else who could. An advocate of a scientific approach to chess who had announced his retirement from the chess arena after losing a match to Tigran Petrosian in the battle for the world championship, but who still participated in tournaments, Botvinnik expressed a readiness to nurture talented young chess players and pass on directly his vast and truly invaluable experience in order to keep the inevitable loss of information to a minimum.

At twelve, I was the youngest candidate for master in the country, and for my entire short chess life I had defended the colors of Trud (insofar as I was a member of a workers' club, even though the overwhelming majority of schoolkids in our country traditionally root for Spartak). In short, according to all the rules of the club I had the right to a place in Botvinnik's school, and I got it.

I was there for three sessions. Since we were all schoolchildren, the sessions were timed to the holidays in autumn, winter, and spring. Our group was made up of many names who have since become famous in chess: Balashov, Dubinskii, Zlotnik, Karpov, Razuvayev, Rashkovskii, and Timoshchenko.

To get an idea of how naïve I still was at that time, suffice it to say that only from my new friends did I learn that *Botvinnik* was Botvinnik's real name. *Tal* was Tal's, and *Korchnoi* was Korchnoi's. For some reason I was sure these were all pseudonyms and that it was common among chess players who had ascended to the upper echelons to conceal their true identities. A unique ritual, so to speak. The reason for this fantasy was probably related more to the fact that these surnames sounded exotic to me, because in Zlatoust one never encountered such names.

At our first meeting Botvinnik made it perfectly clear who we were in relation to him. I don't know if he staged his entrance, since he wouldn't have any need for that, but each word seemed calculated and his whole bearing emphasized his Olympian inaccessibility. He wasn't simply a master who chose the best apprentices from other workshops; he was a god. We were the cho-

sen ones who were lucky enough to have fallen into his
path. We were raw canvasses on which he could casually
lay a daub to impart resiliency and life to the line of the
drawing or succulence to those provincial colors in which
we had been rendered.

In those years Botvinnik took himself too seriously.
He was too much the world champion, too much the
celebrity. His eyes, behind his heavy glasses, were aloof.
During our first lesson he told us that he had begun
work on a computer chess program. In several years this
program would beat not just masters but even grand
masters, and eventually even the world champion wouldn't
stand a chance against it. He said this as if he were challenging us to argue with him. We understood one thing:
The champion had left the arena, but in his place he was
preparing an avenger, a soulless chess murderer to defeat
everyone in the name of its creator.

We were shocked. We didn't see any place for ourselves in the coming chess world which had just opened
up to us as if by magic. If a machine is going to beat all
of us, regardless of the level of talent and strength, then
why bother learning chess at all.

"Don't worry, kids," said Botvinnik. "You'll find work.
After all, my machine will need strong chess player-
programmers. You will be the first."

Our future had already been decided for us. We had
been shown the wheel on which we'd revolve, not daring
to turn off at our own discretion. We'd roll toward the
goal which this massive, tough, and strong person had
chosen for us. Now he was preparing to give each of us
a sufficient push, so the momentum obtained would be
enough to fulfill our historical mission.

That was exactly a quarter century ago.

*   *   *

We didn't come to the first session empty-handed. Each of us had transcriptions of our own games so that it would be easier for Botvinnik to see what he was dealing with. He looked over our games carefully. He had a very particular set of criteria for judging chess talent, a standard which he considered absolute truth, and I didn't fit this pattern at all.

All my games looked approximately alike. Since I had never studied theory, I would fall into an opening game pit from the very first moves. My opponent would dig it out very precisely, according to a variation learned by rote, and when I was sunk, he just as calmly buried me.

Of course, that's how games with experienced opponents played themselves out. I won't talk about games against players as equally inexperienced as myself, because in such cases battles rarely erupted. No matter which color I played—and it was all the same to me—I seized the initiative right off the bat and dealt with my opponent quickly. As these games weren't interesting to me, I didn't think to bring them with me to Moscow. Furthermore, I didn't think they would interest the world champion.

Instead, I brought with me the games that suited my taste, the ones in which there raged real battles, the ones in which there was a real game, at least in my understanding of it. Some said that I only began playing for real when I found myself in deep trouble, but my game began with the first move. I was the only one aware of this at first; not until I was on the razor's edge and could initiate a combination of unique moves would everyone else notice.

My play led me quickly into deep difficulty. My partner

would begin deliberately burying me, but I would try to climb out by setting my back against the wall, dodging the blows, finding unthinkable supports on which to balance, and acting slyly by laying out false retreats. In general, I danced a jig on the head of a pin, drawing my partner out beyond the boundaries of his well-versed variation so that he would have to improvise and not play from memory. I would hold out until he had exhausted all his learned theories and, as victory came into sight, I would lay him out flat. Then, if his position was compromised either strategically or by error, I could clean up with a single blow.

Botvinnik never understood my strategy. He didn't take time to look at it. Some of the other kids in our group got off the hook even easier. The textbook familiarity of their games earned them high marks. I still remember Botvinnik's reaction to each of my games, right from the opening moves. At first he would express amazement, then annoyance, and, finally, irritation. He never looked beyond the fifteenth or twentieth move of my games, assuming he already knew what he'd find there, so when he evaluated me with one of his assistants, Yurkov, Botvinnik said, "The boy doesn't have a clue about chess, and there's no future at all for him in this profession."

This pronouncement, which Yurkov tried to break to me gently, was naturally insulting, but it didn't have a lasting effect on me. The ambitions which Botvinnik had in mind didn't interest me. The only goal he thought worthy—the title of world champion—and for which our school served as a springboard hadn't even entered my mind.

I didn't look further than the dream of gaining the

title of master. I didn't picture myself as even a grand master, to say nothing of aspiring to the chess crown. This was not because I was timid—I wasn't—but because I simply lived in one world, and the grand masters existed in a completely different one. People like that were not really even people, but like gods or mythical heroes.

I was a little twelve year old then who had just stopped playing war with the chess pieces. I couldn't imagine myself as an opponent for the chess Olympians. Besides, my life was filled with many other things, which were just as good as chess: reading books, playing games in our courtyard, and numerous card games. I participated in school, city, regional, and republic Olympiads in subjects from mathematics to geography, and finished each year with honors.

I wasn't prepared to think of chess as work, something that Botvinnik repeated at each of our meetings. He equated it with the highest achievements, but since I had no lofty aspirations, I tuned out his sermons. This isn't for me, I thought, convinced that chess would always be just a game to me.

But still, at Botvinnik's chess school, it was chess day and night, chess without end. I had never had the opportunity to play to my heart's content. Back then we didn't think about serious playing. "Blitz," or lightning chess, ruled among us. Each day the number of games played reached three figures. I soon discovered that if I battled the other kids day and night with moderate success, then sometime around midnight I became unbeatable. At first the kids decided this was coincidence. Then they attributed my late-night victories to physical stamina and began to battle me "scientifically." While one group tried to beat me, the other group was catching up on sleep.

But I still beat them all, sometimes not leaving my chair until at least six in the morning.

Still, a person has to sleep sometime, and we usually made up sleep at the expense of getting up on time. It didn't always work out—on one occasion, we hadn't seen Botvinnik for three days and felt completely carefree, but on the fourth day, following another sleepless night, we woke up around eleven o'clock to a loud knocking at the door. Immediately we knew it was our mentor, but we were all bleary-eyed and unwashed, and breakfast had long since passed. We didn't even try to explain ourselves. Botvinnik wouldn't listen to excuses. We had broken the rules, which allowed him to draw sweeping and unpleasant conclusions about our fates.

That evening we were right back at our never-ending blitz.

CHAPTER THREE

 MEANWHILE, our family life gradually changed for the better. When Father became senior shift engineer at the metallurgical factory, we moved out of our communal apartment into a separate two-room apartment in the same building. That same autumn he traveled to Gagra on the Black Sea to rest. I remember how he refused and didn't want to go ("This trip will put a big hole in our budget") but his health, after a year and a half of study in Moscow, had deteriorated. He tired quickly and was sick often. It was a family decision that he should go.

Father's trip was an event for Zlatoust. Today vacationing at the sea is common, but back then it smacked of elitism. We were even talked about in the city. Other kids in the courtyard asked Larisa and me what Father wrote from there and how he was resting. He brought back stones from the sea—smooth, pale Black Sea pebbles that took on color when wet.

I saw the sea when I turned ten. Before that I fulfilled the norm for the first ranking, and I was sent to Borovichi, a small village between Moscow and Leningrad, to participate in the junior championship of the Russian

Republic. Conditions there couldn't have been worse. There were ten people to a room; we were fed however and whenever; and to take a shower was virtually impossible. The other participants in the tournament were almost twice my age, but they looked after me as best they could. To avoid having to stand through my games, I came to the tournament hall with a large pillow, which I placed on my seat, but even then I was barely visible from behind the board.

Over the years, when journalists and chess fans ask me what role did specialized literature play in my development as a chess player, I usually answer, "A big one," and then proceed to name books which, in my view, any chess novice should study. My list has changed over time, but one book I was exposed to has always figured into it without fail: *The Selected Games of Capablanca*, compiled by Vasily Panov. I added to my praise for the book personal experiences and became so well-rehearsed at doing this that, soon after, every article about me contained a discussion on how I have been influenced by Capablanca's style, how our games are similarly constructed around an accumulation of small advantages, with the culmination of battle transferred to the endgame. Moreover, the culmination can seem wholly imperceptible to the average fan—in short, flat and pragmatic. I never bothered to argue with the articles.

I don't claim that with my style of play I tried to refute such commentaries. I simply played as I could and as the circumstances permitted. I love a sharp game and I will gladly embrace it when it is the most reasonable way to solve problems on the chessboard. But to force a game just because it might seem more exciting—that would be foolish. I have to rely on my own tastes, on a classical style. Capablanca didn't discover it, and I didn't perfect it, but both of us are masters of this school where, beyond the simplicity of the drawing and the clarity of the lines, lie hidden depths with a colossal energy. This is why it's never boring to look at a genuinely classical game. Its translucency makes it possible to dive as deeply as you can bear, but if you come back to it and dive even deeper, you will discover new depths and new perspectives.

So, then, I don't deny Capablanca's influence or the influence of Alekhine, Tal, Fischer, and Spassky. Each chess player has his own personality and inevitably influences you with his games, acting upon your understanding of chess. There is nothing shameful or dangerous about this, as long as your own style has already formed. In doing so, you're discovering yourself by using another master's key. In knowing him, you come to know yourself.

It might be appropriate here to recall my old friend from childhood, Sasha Kolyshkin. Many times, when I went to visit him, I found him painstakingly poring over the games of Alekhine or Tchigorin. Unlike mine, his attitude to chess was extraordinarily serious. He analyzed it, scrutinized it, and learned it by heart. Yet he never made it in the chess profession, even though he was given the same tools as I was. I know, because I played hundreds of games against him. His excessive thoroughness and bookishness destroyed his integrity and compromised his individuality. Back then I didn't have the chance to help him. I only had a feeling that he was on the wrong path. The only thing he ever heard from me was something like "Sanya, stop beating your brains.

Let's play blitz instead." I wasn't being lazy—I was trying to protect myself from his methodical studies.

In my life, I have seen many like him—hopelessly in love with chess—at all levels, right up to the grandmasters. All of them had their wings clipped by conventional chess wisdom. Even Gary Kasparov, with his ceaseless studying and industriousness, triumphed in spite of this terrible machine which tried to grind him up.

In spite of my early training, I learned not to play by rote, to borrow blindly, or take everything on trust. By all means examine the games of the great chess players, but don't swallow them whole. Their games are valuable not for their separate moves, but for their vision of chess, their way of thinking.

You have to trust your intuition to help you find the right resources for your needs, as well as to tell you when to stop, when to pause and digest what you've learned. I wasn't that lucky. I didn't have someone to give me that advice. There was no one whose counsel I unconditionally believed, and the example of my friends, who studied theory and texts, didn't inspire me. I felt they were misguided. In any event, I didn't doubt that I needed something totally and completely different, but I didn't know what. Unfortunately, I met my Teacher too late for him to instill in me a taste for working with specialized literature.

My relationship to my first chess books was such that I didn't distinguish them from other books. On the contrary, I preferred the usual books of most young boys: science fiction, spy and criminal adventures, tales of journeys to exotic lands, and, of course, books about war. I even collected soldiers' and officers' memoirs, distinguishing the technical aspects of the troops: pilots, tank drivers, and artillerymen.

It never even occurred to me to collect chess books. I didn't attach any significance to them, but naturally these books found their way to my shelves. Many people knew of my tournament successes and if they happened to come across a chess book, they would send it to me.

My first chess book, which I got soon after I joined the chess club, was Panov's *Course of Openings*. A modest book that had no other aim than to acquaint devotees with the rudiments of opening strategy, it didn't leave any trace in my memory. I would open it for basic information, but that's it. The second book was *The Selected Games of Capablanca,* also compiled by Panov. Father gave it to me on my eighth birthday. To this day I am amazed at how easy it was back then to buy such a fantastic book.

I studied this book and read it from cover to cover, like a novel or adventure story. I lived out each game described in it, but I didn't sink my teeth into the text and analyze it. Perhaps that's the reason I remembered this book in all its details. I would read it for enjoyment at bedtime. I read it not because I had to, but because I wanted to; I was learning and studying without realizing it.

In 1963 my father was given a raise and made chief engineer at the South Urals Economic Council (in Western terms, one of the managers at the biggest plant), but one year later Soviet Premier Nikita Khrushchev was removed from power and economic councils across the whole country were dismantled. Hundreds of administrators and specialists, including my father, found themselves out of work. For a while he was listed as deputy director at his former plant. Then he was offered several positions right away. Some of the offers were from the country's largest factories, but Father chose a small plant in Tula. He was motivated not by career prospects, but by the interests of his children. Larisa was preparing to enter the Tula Polytechnic Institute, and with each year I was traveling more frequently to tournaments. All my travels took me through Moscow, which was a short ride on the commuter train to Tula.

In Tula our family finally became materially well-off. In addition to drawing a good salary, Father received regular bonuses. With his arrival the factory began exhibiting stable growth in production. At the same time I also started to become financially self-sufficient.

We have the attitude in our country that schoolchildren should be busy only with schoolwork. They have no opportunity to earn money, and the laws as they're written don't do anything to encourage it. With highschool students it's somewhat different. They have the right to make an extra ruble on the side, but the majority of them live off their parents for the duration of their studies. Good grades are encouraged by stipends, but they are small change.

I didn't lack for anything at home, but the stamp collection I had gradually grew into a passion. This hobby didn't come cheaply, and although my parents never refused me anything, I wouldn't let myself ask for more than three rubles a month for stamps. As this small amount was never enough, I refused myself everything, and if some pocket change did come my way, I managed it extremely frugally.

Now you get an idea of the freedom I found when I became a master of sport in 1966. From that time on I had the chance to make a living from chess, despite the paltry sums involved. Our chess journals pay little, and I would receive only ten rubles for a simultaneous exhibition. But from that day, when I earned my first ten rubles, I never again begged for stamp money, yet I limited myself in simultaneous exhibitions to the bare minimum wage needed for my stamp collection to survive. It never even occurred to me to try to earn more or to have extra money in my pocket.

Even then my view of chess as a source of material wealth was close to indifference. That attitude eventually became the following rule: Don't turn anything down, but don't do anything more than is necessary. You might say it's the philosophy of a lazy person, but I don't agree. I believe that a person can derive satisfaction from contemplating accumulated riches and even from thoughts about them. However, I get basic joy from completely different, simple things like the sea, a sunny autumn day spent outside Moscow, conversation with a friend, and, finally, a good game of blitz.

When it became possible for me to finance my activities completely, I took immediate advantage of it. I was seventeen and had just finished school, with a gold medal in mathematics. I had to decide about my further schooling and about chess. The Faculty of Mathematics and Mechanics at Moscow State University had been chosen long ago, but there is a huge difference between the words *to choose* and *to enroll,* even with a gold medal.

It was not such an easy thing getting into the university. Although I passed the examinations, I just missed getting accepted. I took my documents with me to

Leningrad, lured there by talk of a very strong chess team at the Institute of Mechanics. Everything turned out to be too difficult and that move didn't occur. My flight from Moscow was found out by the capital's grand-masters. Botvinnik and Smyslov wrote a petition to the Minister of Higher Education, who supported them, and I was put back in place in Moscow State University.

My life at school changed my financial situation—a student stipend is merely a token, and taking money from my parents was out of the question. Earning money from simultaneous exhibitions became a necessity.

There was one other source—I was eligible for a sports stipend, but the question was how to get it. At the time, our sports program was undergoing yet another reorganization. Sports officials were uncertain of their fate from one day to the next and, as a result, confusion and doubt reigned. My own sports society—Trud—seemed secure, but my circumstances and abilities didn't interest anyone. The Armed Forces Club heard of my problem and immediately asked me to join them. Trud let me go, and on the same day I became a member of the Armed Forces Club, a move I've never regretted. They gave me a master's stipend of a hundred rubles, ninety-two of which actually ended up in my hands.

When I became a grandmaster two years later, the stipend was automatically raised by 40 percent to 140 rubles. Two years later, when I was named to the USSR National Team, the USSR Sports Committee gave me a stipend of two hundred rubles.

In addition, there were prizes. The first ones dated back to school days. How can I ever forget the first one, for seventy dollars, for victory in the European Junior

Championship? I can still see those seven worn ten-dollar bills.

Next came first prize in Czechoslovakia at a tournament of young masters: two hundred rubles. For a fifteen-year-old boy, that's quite a sum. I bought Mama shoes (there has always been a shoe shortage in our country) and myself a portable chess set for twenty-six Czech korunas (three rubles then). I still take this set with me on every trip and to every tournament.

This trip also brought me a lasting friendship with an outstanding chess player, Lubomir Kavalek. The trip began with misunderstanding and a setback. The misunderstanding came about when our sports federation, having mistranslated the program, decided that Trshinets was the site for a youth tournament (not a junior tournament, as it was actually written) and sent two youths there: the seventeen-year-old master Kupreichik and me. When it became clear that all the other participants were several years older than we, Kupreichik became frightened. For me, though, it was no different from what I had been used to my whole life. Kupreichik eventually got a hold of himself, too.

The setback was also technical. On the day of our departure for Moscow there was a heavy snowstorm that lasted three days, making it impossible to get out of town. When we finally made it to Prague, the tournament had already begun and no one had any need for two children. The train for Trshinets left in the evening, and we were stuck with a whole day in a strange city in a strange land.

Fortunately, Lubomir Kavalek had some free time and spent it on us. He met us in his car and drove us around

Prague, fed us, took us to a movie, and so on, right up until the time of the train for Trshinets. This grown man, an international grandmaster entertaining two unknown national masters, was so benevolent and courteous that for many years afterward the word *Czech* meant hospitality to me. I can imagine, for example, how Petrosian would have reacted if Lubash had come to Moscow that year, and he were asked to greet the guest and spend a whole day with him. He'd probably decide that someone was playing a practical joke, or wanted to humiliate him. "What, waste my free time on some Kavalek?!"

The fate of my friend was not an easy one. After the "Prague Spring" he was forced to leave the country, but no matter in what direction life threw him, or how the political situation has changed, his place in my heart remains firm. Although more than twenty years have passed since that wintry Prague day, I still feel indebted to Lubash.

I'll never forget the famous Moscow "all-star" tournament which entered chess history as the Alekhine Memorial Tournament. The best grandmasters of the world took part in it, with the exception of Fischer and the Dane, Bent Larsen. In this illustrious company I shared victory with the late Leonid Shtein. On the occasion of my success, Korchnoi remarked poisonously, "Everyone participated, but not everyone played. The honor, of course, is nice, but nicer still is a worthy prize. You call this a prize, this pittance the organizers offered us? If there had been some real money in the kitty, then there would have been a different level of playing. Then they would have seen what place Karpov ends up in. He's going abroad for a tournament where the money is decent, and then everything will immediately fall into its proper place."

What's true is true. First prize for the grandiose Alekhine Memorial was more than modest: two thousand rubles. It didn't take long to disprove Korchnoi. In several days I was to face a test in the annual Hastings Tournament. Ironically, I was sent there along with Korchnoi. We shared first prize, each of us getting around a thousand dollars. I was waiting to hear what he might say next, but Viktor Lvovich, pacified by his victory over me in a personal encounter, was condescending and looked at me as if from on high. His look seemed to say that, although we arrived even at the finish, the game between us separated the men from the boys.

A few days remained after the completion of the tournament until our departure, and the organizers asked us to travel around the country playing simultaneous exhibitions. I've already said that I try not to abuse this form of earning money, but here the conditions offered were belittling—one pound per board. Even then it was no secret that Soviet chess players were not rich, to put it mildly, and the organizers had no doubt we would jump at this chance. I was about to refuse, but Viktor Lvovich explained to me with his malicious smile, "Tolya, you calculate poorly. One pound each for ten boards is only ten pounds. But if there aren't ten boards, but sixty, then it's already a whole sixty pounds for the same amount of time practically, for the same work."

And he contracted to play every day, maybe more than once a day, I don't know. I agreed to three small exhibitions on the condition that the organizers first show me the cities where I had agreed to play: Newcastle,

Leicester, and, of course, London. I looked at England and the English people with pleasure, and although toward the end I was exhausted, it was a pleasurable fatigue. I was stunned to see Korchnoi on the day of departure—tormented, with a feverish glow in his eyes, barely alive. His luggage was unliftable, about five times heavier than mine, and I wasn't leaving England empty-handed either; I bought my first stereo system there.

"Don't worry," chuckled Korchnoi. "We'll get it there. Remember this: The level of a grandmaster is determined by his luggage."

"I visited museums—" I began to say, but Korchnoi didn't let me finish. He burst out laughing.

"You're a real oddball, Tolya! I've traveled abroad for so many years now, and you're the first grandmaster I've ever met who doesn't dash straightaway to a store, but to a museum. Did you lose something there?"

He was right, unfortunately. I myself have been traveling around the world for twenty years, and I have never met a chess player who would agree to join me for a visit to an art gallery. In 1974, after the Twenty-first Chess Olympiad in Nice, Petrosian and I went to Paris. Prior to this, neither of us had ever been to the Louvre. I tried to talk him into going, and I succeeded. But the following day (no doubt after having been worked over by his wife, Rona), he refused.

"Why do we need the Louvre when the stores are much more interesting?"

"What are you talking about! If the Mona Lisa were the only thing there, I'd still walk across all of Paris to get a look at her."

"I don't get it. Why?" repeated Petrosian. "So you look at her—big deal. If you don't see her, what have you lost? You want to tell people in Moscow you were in the Louvre? So tell them. Who's going to check up on it? You were in Paris. They'll believe you." Unbelievably proud of his line of reasoning, he took Rona by the arm and set out for Galeries Lafayette.

The year 1971 was a critical one because of Bobby Fischer. Thanks to his successes, businesslike efficiency, and pressure, the chess circuit was saturated with so much money that to this day we continue to enjoy the fruits of his efforts. True, the peak passed a long time ago. In 1975 the Philippines offered a purse of five million dollars for a match between Fischer and myself, but the prize fund for the last world championship match in Seville was "only" two million dollars. I put quotation marks around *only* because it's the largest award in the history of chess (the much-anticipated Philippines match never took place).

But 1968 was my turning point. I started to live on my own, I changed clubs, and I found a coach. This was the year Semyon Abramovich Furman entered my life.

I had already seen him once before, when I was twelve, at a study and training session of Trud's chess players. At that time a match was being played for the world championship between Botvinnik and Petrosian. It was to be Botvinnik's last match. Furman was one of his assistants and after the game had been adjourned in a tough position (Botvinnik thought he should have gained the upper hand), he gave an evaluation that was unexpected for the rest of the team: "We have to find a draw." "We're going to look only for victory," Botvinnik demanded. The situation in the match led him to believe this, and all the assistants supported him. Only Furman said, "First show me a draw."

This was his rule, and it later became mine as well: If the game is adjourned in an unclear position, if the position can't be read right away, if there is no simple analysis of it that says victory, then first find a draw. Countless times I've seen chess players, seduced by outward appearances and first impressions, look for victory right up to the last minute, only to be forced to concede their error in judgment. This has brought many unnecessary defeats. It's not easy to be pragmatic—a player by nature is optimistic and won't give up.

But Semyon Abramovich was principled, firm, and unwavering when it came to his convictions. Botvinnik didn't like this independence, and banished Furman to give lectures to the youthful Trud chess players, who had assembled outside Moscow. Two days later he demanded him back: Semyon Abramovich turned out to be right. The game could not be saved.

Furman didn't notice me at that session, and that's to be expected. I was little both in size and age and, although I was bright, I couldn't pretend to be anything more than a curiosity to him. But Furman astounded me with his chess depth, a depth which he revealed easily and naturally, as if all he were doing was establishing already well-known truths. He astounded me—it was as if he were reading my own thoughts. But I could only guess at strategy—I didn't have the ability to think it through. Furman had thought everything through to the end, condensing it into crystal-clear thoughts. It was as though he took me by the hand, and I moved everywhere he went. My eyes opened.

The second meeting with him was not to take place for another six years, again at a study-training session, before the USSR Team Championship.

At first I didn't recognize him. He had once seemed youthful, with a head of thick black hair, strong, and cheerful. Now I saw before me an aging and tired person who moved slowly and spoke reluctantly. His hair had thinned and grayed, and his eyes had lost their spark. I remembered the old Furman and the impression he had made upon me, the feeling of recognizing in him my own vision and thoughts and everything else that had astounded me as a twelve year old. All that couldn't have disappeared without a trace—it had to be there, somewhere.

Only a year later did I learn that, not long before that second encounter, Furman had undergone an extremely difficult operation. He had stomach cancer, and though the doctors assured him that the operation had gone smoothly, they didn't conceal from him the fact that only time would tell if it was successful. If he held on for five years, he would live a long time, they told him. This second meeting wasn't as striking as the first. Furman had lost his presence and stature. Still, he was attentive, analytic, at times sharp, and full of ideas—in short an unextraordinary but solid chess specialist. Good and conscientious, but nothing more.

I won't say I was disappointed. Even then I wasn't inclined to reach hasty conclusions. I simply tried to understand. He and I had ended up in the same club, and that was a good sign. But I didn't have any far-reaching plans, because so far I was nobody in chess, yet Furman—even a tired Furman—was still a specialist who helped the world's best chess players. I still had a lot of growing to do before I'd be fully worthy of his attention and on equal footing with him.

But he took note of me. There were joint analyses and we played as equals in speed chess. In the tournament for which we had been preparing, I performed excellently. Out of nine games, I won seven with two draws. When, half a year later, he was asked to help prepare me for the World Junior Championship in Stockholm, he willingly consented.

I requested that he be invited to work with me. Juniors usually don't get asked with whom they'd like to train, and even my selection had been preceded by an unbecoming behind-the-scenes battle. Prominent chess authorities tried to block me. It was difficult to get them to observe sports principle, and even when I managed to get past this, they continued to make my life difficult. When I was finally in, I was still prepared for the worst, expecting dirty tricks from all sides. When the question came up about a coach who would prepare me for the World Junior Championship, I realized that I had to make the selection myself and insist upon it. I also realized that the main virtue of this coach should not be knowledge or experience, but decency, because I was surrounded by treachery. I wanted to be absolutely certain of the person who was going to help me. That's why I chose Furman.

They explained to me that it was not the same Furman, that cancer had cut him down, that after the operation he had withdrawn entirely into himself, and that when a person is indifferent to the world around him, there's not much that can be expected of him. None of this dissuaded me. I remembered the old Furman, I believed that an interesting assignment would invigorate him, give him added strength, and help him return to his former self.

He began working with me at a deliberate pace, attempting to glean from our conversation my character and values. Together we looked at my games, but as if from above, not the way it's usually done. In this way a game acquired a depth before our eyes. With this framework, Furman established criteria and immediately all my poorly considered moves became obvious. We analyzed everything that happened around each of them, trying to see where they came from, and what made me choose them.

Finally, we turned our attention to chess openings. This is where Furman had no equals, which was fitting since I was a dilettante when it came to the opening game.

We understood that my future opponents, with the strength of their youth, were going to use sharp games and tactics. In this sense I hardly differed from them. But I also preferred a precise positional game, and Furman proposed accentuating the positional game with strategy to counter opponents. The plan turned out to be a good one.

Although Furman put little faith in success (his cancer had made him a pessimist), I managed, though not without difficulty, to win in Stockholm. This enlivened Semyon Abramovich. He felt a change in himself, but saw that I was the catalyst for this change. He recharged himself with my energy, which gave him back the assurance and optimism the disease had crushed. He asked me to assist him in the national championship.

Sadly, this tournament did not decorate him with laurels. He overestimated his strength to get through a whole game. What surprised me, though, was his mono-chromatic approach. I already knew that Furman was "the world champion at playing White," but Furman turned an ostensibly minor whim—the right to move first—into a weapon of astounding force. This happened in part due to his brilliant knowledge, but also because of a striking perception of the opening game which he artistically played out with the white pieces. The first moves in his hands turned into a victorious handicap, negating any efforts by even his biggest-name opponents.

But when he was handed the black pieces it was as if a completely different person replaced Semyon Abramovich. He didn't even try to hide his annoyance at having to deal with such a hopeless situation. Naturally, he tried to dig in his heels for battle, but he was so despondent that it immediately became clear only a miracle could save him.

For me, this was a good lesson. It would have been difficult to think up a more convincing argument in favor of "two-coloredness" or "two-handedness," or whatever you choose to call it. I saw that if I wanted to get some-where in chess, I would have to overcome the problem of playing Black. I became convinced for the first time of the great role psychology plays in chess. With his talent, knowledge, and mastery, Furman could have fully resist-ed the strongest chess players of the world with the black pieces. While preparing for games I became convinced on numerous occasions that his responses to the most unexpected plans of White were excellent. His problem was that he didn't suffer losses *during* a game, but before it. He single-handedly created his own destruction.

*   *   *

I consider Furman to have been my coach from the days when he helped me prepare for the World Junior Championship because he immediately brought new vision and new depth to my approach to chess. It was as if he introduced me to the university of chess. A new phase in mastering chess had begun for me. I'm not simply indebted to Furman for this, but, because of it, I became attached to him.

Later, looking back on it, Furman calculated our joint destiny from even earlier periods and said this so often to journalists that he began believing it himself. The reality was different. The initial experiences of working with me were passing episodes for him. Interesting, but only episodes. After all, Furman was a specialist who helped the greatest chess fighters in the world. I was a new international master, but he hadn't noticed me. "He undoubtedly will become a grand master," Furman remarked about me, "but as to how his chess fate will develop further, it's too early to say."

In addition, we lived far from one another: I in Moscow, he in Leningrad. Constant contact was virtually out of the question, and he was preoccupied with helping Korchnoi prepare for the next candidates' tournament.

I applied myself to my university studies, especially since the lessons took up so much time. They weren't so difficult as they were laborious. I hadn't suspected that I would have to shovel mountains of material just to manufacture skills. This was my first bout of disillusionment with my chosen profession.

From time to time I participated in tournaments. Ambition didn't drive me, but this wasn't a reason to postpone the struggle for the title of grandmaster. And

I bided my time, waiting to play in a tournament for the grandmaster norm.

After I returned from Stockholm as the world junior champion, I didn't make grand plans concerning my future chess career because I knew that my success wouldn't open a single bureaucrat's door. If you belong to a certain group or if someone takes an interest in you, then all your problems are solved. If you're on your own, then many obstacles appear on what should be a simple road. And that's exactly the situation I found myself in: a greenhorn in Moscow, a greenhorn in the Armed Forces Club, and a bumpkin to boot, but self-sufficient and with backbone, which rubs some people the wrong way. I didn't want a guide to follow blindly along on a leash. I preferred to choose my own road and companions.

While my success was still recent, I asked our sports committee to allow me to play in a tournament at the grandmaster level. I didn't have designs on the big tournaments. They found a tournament for me in Holland in ten months. It sounds like a long time to wait, but, as I said before, I was in no hurry.

I didn't deceive myself by expecting a smooth beginning, understanding that naturally there would be difficulties. It turned out that such difficulties weren't even needed. Life was much simpler and crueler. A few months before the tournament, the world champion, Boris Spassky, began eyeballing it. Places were still available. Spassky joined the team, ennobling the tournament with his presence. Spassky was the first to see me as a truly dangerous opponent. He didn't try to hurt me—but he did take advantage of a situation that slowed me down. "In order to prepare for the upcoming match with the challenger, it is necessary that my coach Geller travel with me to Holland," he said. That was enough to get me bumped from the tournament and have my place taken by Geller.

Every cloud has a silver lining. It just so happened that right at this time the organizers of the Caracas Tournament (it was called the President's Cup because the president of Venezuela himself was overseeing it) tried to prevail upon our sports committee to get Spassky and Petrosian for themselves. As none of our chess players had been in Venezuela, they had no idea what the conditions there were like, so they refused. Then the organizers requested Leonid Shtein and me, the national champion and world junior champion. Again our bureaucrats refused, simply not wanting to bother themselves with it all. Only the personal intercession of the Venezuelan president, who made a phone call to our premier, Kosygin, broke the deadlock. The matter was resolved instantly. As the tournament was about to get under way any day now, Shtein and I were shoved onto the plane without completing the usual paperwork. Our documents, including our visas, caught up with us in Paris.

With a little more experience, I could have won this tournament. I was in front for a long time, but as the feeling of danger lessened I blundered away an assured victory over Ivkov. This shook me up so much that I began to "space out" and miss attacks. Only toward the end did I collect my game again. The breakdown not only cost me victory, but even a prizewinning place in the overall finish. But the goal had been accomplished: I fulfilled the requirements and became the youngest grandmaster in the world.

*   *   *

At the same time Furman and Korchnoi were having their disagreements.

It wasn't so easy to quarrel with Semyon Abramovich. Mild and urbane, he preferred compromise to arguments. It took a Korchnoi to get Furman riled up. In the quarterfinal (played in Amsterdam, where Furman had accompanied Korchnoi), the chess veteran Reshevsky had been demolished. The next match was to be against Geller, who, like Furman, was in the Armed Forces Club. Semyon Abramovich, punctilious in the extreme concerning questions of morality, decided that this circumstance prevented him from being Korchnoi's second in their match.

"I can play a fellow club member only personally, only at the board," he said. "Otherwise I won't be properly understood. Moreover, Geller and I have worked together many times in the past, and I know his preparations. This is all the more reason why I can't help his opponent. In short, there is no alternative to this solution. My reputation is worth more than any success."

Korchnoi was enraged! He thought Furman's reasoning was laughable. "The other way around!" he said. "It is a gift that you know Geller's methods. It will be that much easier to win. And winners aren't judged."

It can't be said this came as any surprise to Furman. He knew Korchnoi, respected him as a chess player, and tolerated him as a person. This time, though, it was not a matter of Korchnoi's morals, but of Furman's own conscience. He replied with a firm no. Then he added, "Don't fool yourself. You're stronger than Geller and will beat him without my help. Afterward I'll come back to you, and we'll continue working together to prepare for the final match."

Korchnoi wouldn't hear of it and took a wholly unprecedented step. He began putting pressure on Furman through the news and television media. This belief in the power of public opinion is Korchnoi's weakness. The effect of his action was exactly contrary to what he intended. Furman simply said, "Viktor, I'll thank you never to turn to me for help again."

Attacked in any other case, Korchnoi would have refused him help. It didn't happen here for one reason: Korchnoi continued to hope that Furman, if he were offered an interesting assignment, say a match with Fischer, would still be willing to help. Such a match never came about, but I didn't waste any time. Upon learning that there was a spot next to Furman available, I immediately tried to fill it. I even moved to Leningrad and transferred from Moscow State University to Leningrad State University.

After one year's study in Moscow, I realized that I had to make a choice between mathematics and chess. Mathematics was beginning to interest me less and less. I didn't like it nearly as much as I had in high school, most likely because I couldn't commit to it wholeheartedly. I had to ask the question point-blank: What is it I can't live without? The answer was immediate and given without hesitation: chess.

The leadership of the student chess club at Moscow State University decided it wanted me and made me an offer to leave the Armed Forces Club and join them. I wasn't even interested. They began to pressure me, but I stood my ground. Then they said: Fine, since you're so stubborn, you have only yourself to blame. And soon after I sensed how this threat was becoming reality. My teachers began to find fault with every little thing. If I wanted to take an exam or quiz ahead of schedule (in order to get in a tournament on time), they refused.

By this time all I needed was the slightest push to leave. I traveled to Leningrad to celebrate the New Year. During my stay there Korchnoi introduced me to one of his childhood friends, a Professor Lavrov. I told him about my lack of interest in mathematics and about the badgering I was experiencing at Moscow.

"That's no good," the professor announced resolutely. "You won't last long like that. You'll consume yourself with unhappiness and negative emotions. You have to live freely and contentedly."

"What should I do?" I asked.

"Come to us. I guarantee you the most favorable regimen. But mathematics here is the same as there. It doesn't get any different from a change of scenery."

I had already thought about this.

"What if it were possible to transfer to the economics department?"

It turned out that it was.

The most amusing thing about this is that Korchnoi had a certain hand in my move to Leningrad. The reason for his goodwill wasn't difficult to guess: He didn't take me seriously. Never once did he consider that in a few short years I could become his competition. Perhaps it was blindness, caused by conceit. But for a player of that class, he was an astoundingly bad judge of danger.

CHAPTER FOUR

MY ASSOCIATION WITH KORCHNOI is linked with many difficult moments, dark thoughts, disappointments, and despair, but I have nothing against Korchnoi. He is the way he is, and I always accepted him as such. I tried to understand, and even forgive, him for all the bad things he did to me and, although it's very difficult, I have no animosity for him. Instead, there is pity and regret. Had he been different, not so quarrelsome and cynical, his life would have been much happier. My regret is for Korchnoi the person. As far as Korchnoi the chess player is concerned, he fulfilled himself as much as his strength and talent allowed.

In chess he attained everything, except for the world championship. It wasn't his lot. At first he seemed to just be biding his time, but later it turned out he was not as strong as Spassky or Petrosian. And when he surpassed them, I appeared on the scene. These were his best years, but I grew faster than he did in strength. I am adamant about this, because I have heard so many times that Korchnoi had the great misfortune of meeting me when his best playing was already behind him. Nothing of the sort! Korchnoi's best years arrived exactly at the time he battled me, but I was mightier and proved this right away, asserting my superiority many, many times thereafter. I confirmed it with my playing, and in battle. It's amazing to me that to this day he can't understand that it wasn't people or circumstances, but chess, that judged us.

I first saw Korchnoi at a simultaneous exhibition which he gave at the Palace of Culture of a tractor factory, when I was ten years old. As the number of people who wanted to play was great, Sasha Kolyshkin and I sat at one board. From a short and not entirely coherent speech he gave before the exhibition, I understood only that no one in chess nowadays knew how to play seriously, that rote memorization and immorality were rampant, and that he, Korchnoi, could have achieved much more if misfortune and unscrupulous opponents, whom he didn't choose, hadn't stood in his way.

He didn't have to worry about ambition. He composed himself and moved the pieces energetically. His face smiled, but a poisonous and malicious joy swam in his eyes. He liked to show off his prowess, and liked to annihilate helpless opponents. In the game with us he played the Scottish Opening, surprising both Sasha and me when he returned his bishops to their places after having developed all his pieces and then placed his rooks in the center. All the same, we figured out his intentions and, when we had neutralized them, we accepted Korchnoi's offer of a draw.

Three or four years later I saw him again. It was in Podol'sk, at a junior training session. He had little to say about chess ideas or trends. Instead, he tried to get us to like him by relating scabrous chess stories and anecdotes. And once again he complained of his fate and the low morals ruling at the highest chess levels. For the first time, I heard the details about the plot at the candidates' tournament in Curaçao among the grandmasters Geller, Keres, and Petrosian who, for the sake of economizing their strength, quietly shared their points. Korchnoi's indignation was understandable but we, his young audience, weren't unanimous in our estimation of him. We concluded that all of Korchnoi's damnation was brought about solely by the fact that the conspirators hadn't invited him into their camp.

Korchnoi never occupied my imagination. His vision of how to construct and play a game was foreign to me. I sense brute force in it. I never wanted to imitate him. For me, he was simply a fact of chess life, an incomprehensible and—to be honest—not very interesting person. For me, he existed only when I looked at his games.

So I was completely calm and unintimidated during our first meeting. Of course, I had an idea of how high his worth was, but I also knew my own value.

The meeting took place not long before the World Junior Championship. My coach, Furman, said, "Let's make a trip to see Korchnoi. He's excellent at speed chess and, besides, it would be a good thing for you to get to know him."

And off we went to the rest home Dyuna, located outside Leningrad, where Korchnoi used to go with his wife, Bela.

He greeted us with a contempt that barely passed indifference. For the first few minutes he hardly noticed me. After all, who was I to him—just a shabby kid, freshly baked provincial master, the kind our chess federation stamps out every year in large quantities. Maybe only in a bad dream could he have seen then my future status as rival.

Like dogs who sniff each other when meeting, chess players have a ritual at first acquaintance: they sit down to play speed chess. And we were not about to violate it—we sat down immediately. I scored right off the bat. This is understandable, because at such a meeting you muster all your strength and hit forcefully and accurately. Korchnoi didn't realize right away that this was not an accident, but an indication of my level of play. After two or three more games that he couldn't turn around, his nature took over, making him wild. He stood over the board, seeing nothing except the pieces and banging them down so hard that all the other pieces jumped. He withdrew completely into chess, focusing all his energy and will on it. And he got what he was after: the initiative clearly went over to his side and he started outplaying me. Besides, I began to take something off my game, thinking that if it was important for him, I'd let him beat me.

Here Furman interceded. Seizing an opportunity when Korchnoi had stepped away from the board for a minute, he whispered, "Tolya, you see what time it is?" It was going on midnight. "If you want to get a ride back in the car, you *have* to win."

That's how I came to know that Korchnoi respects only those who are stronger than he. So I, too, began to play at full tilt and broke my opponent's momentum. I began to win game after game, without conceding a single one. It was just like being back in Botvinnik's school—no one was my equal after midnight.

When Korchnoi had grown sick of playing, Bela gave us a ride back in the Volga.

*   *   *

Exactly one year later we played our first serious game at my first national championship. Right from the opening I found myself in the toughest situations. At the cost of incredible tension, I almost equaled our positions, but I didn't have the muscle to hold on, and I lost.

In analyzing the moves of my opponent, I understood that before games with Korchnoi, it wasn't to my advantage to rely upon Furman's advice on openings. During the years of their collaboration Korchnoi had studied Furman and almost unerringly guessed not only his opening, but also the ramification by which the game would progress. But he never caught me by surprise again because, after listening to my coach, I acted on my own. My choice didn't necessarily deviate from Furman's advice and, in fact, it could even correspond to it, but in such an event I had to know where Korchnoi would set a trap for me and then turn off at least one move in advance. When I succeeded in doing this, I deprived Korchnoi of his "rightful" opening superiority.

Incidentally, these miscalculations with Korchnoi illustrate two of the most important facets of Furman's personality. First, his ingenuousness—he knew his favorite strategies, yet he wouldn't make use of this knowledge in the fight against him. Just as he refused to fight one-on-one with Geller, he couldn't take advantage of someone's confidence. Second, and this seems to have been a consequence of the first, chess for Furman was limited to the chessboard. He played against the pieces, never against the person. He sought truth only on the chessboard. The human factor, in any form, only stayed him from his goal. His disregard for psychology deprived him of serious sports success, but he won a lot of fans with his quixotic pure idealism.

*   *   *

But I still had to win, not speculatively, but against flesh-and-blood opponents with the same ambition as mine, and the capability of doing anything for the sake of winning. I didn't single out Korchnoi among them until right before our first match. But I took psychology into account and by our next official game, at the Alekhine Memorial, I had my revenge.

Korchnoi turned to stone. I already knew how he acted after a defeat, and expected something much worse, but he simply stopped acknowledging me. Later he realized how silly this was. At a tournament, after all, the participants are constantly bumping into each other, and so he changed his tactics. He began to kid me, needle me, and make sarcastic remarks. If he had been my peer, I would have quickly retaliated in kind, but he was twice my age and he was *Korchnoi*. How could I treat him like just another difficult opponent?

When the Memorial ended with my victory, Korchnoi couldn't pass up the chance to disparage me with the remarks I mentioned earlier: In effect, let Karpov win in a tournament where the stakes are decent. He knew what he was talking about. Just a few days later, we traveled together to England for the traditional Hastings Tournament. This was Korchnoi's challenge to me: Let's see if you can get around me when I play for money.

I think that if he had soberly analyzed my game, he wouldn't have been so arrogant. Even then my game contained all the elements of my future winning style. If Korchnoi had studied my game rationally and calmly he would have seen this. But when Korchnoi got wound up, and especially when he began talking, he was unable to see things clearly.

Maybe the money overexcited him, or he lost his form; maybe he tried too hard, but his game derailed and he couldn't get it back on track. With me it was just the opposite: everything I tried worked. I easily led the tournament, racking up point after point.

Korchnoi avoided me at the tournament. He walked away from my conversations, his eyes averted. Sometimes, I caught him glaring at me with venom. He stored up strength and malice and when it finally came time for our own game, his agitation had peaked. He played as if his life depended on it. He put everything he had into it, and won. Instantly he changed, becoming arrogant and condescending. And the worse I did in the tournament (I got so hung up on my loss to Korchnoi that I couldn't get myself back in form), the more magnanimous he became. Even when I caught up to him in the final round and we shared victory, he wasn't that upset, because he had asserted his superiority over me in *our* meeting.

This game which again put him ahead in our personal score was important to Korchnoi. Before that, Korchnoi and I had played a closed practice match. But this was a real match, consisting of six games. He was testing his readiness before his match with Geller, the match in which Furman refused to take part.

We played at Korchnoi's place. I still didn't have a roof over my head, and I was busy running around, following the proper procedures and trying to figure out who was keeping me from getting the apartment promised me.

This dragged on for months. Here is where I learned the rules of this strange system in which a petty bureaucrat can ignore any instructions, even if they come down from the director of a huge and powerful department. I could write a satirical novel about this apartment episode, but I'll pass over this story, which now seems funny, although back then I failed to see anything humorous about it. It didn't embitter or devastate me, although it easily could have. I have seen so many people broken by this, but for me it was a lesson in the psychology of the lone bureaucrat and the whole hierarchy.

Korchnoi dictated the conditions of the match. He would play Black for all the games (he had to check his skills there) and he would also determine the openings to be used. Finally, an adjourned game was to be played out in the same day, after a short break for lunch.

I remember the first opening used was the Ruy Lopez. I love this opening, and I think I know and feel it pretty well. So far the mood was good, and the playing went smoothly and enjoyably. In general, I was leading toward the break. This was obvious when I looked at Korchnoi, who had become very moody. He didn't like the looks of things at all. I had no specific plan for asserting my superiority, but I didn't doubt I would. When the match resumed I'd sit and think awhile, and then I'd find the right way.

We repaired to the kitchen to eat. I have enjoyed his wife's cooking many times since that day, but on this occasion Bela was not in top form. One look at the plate was enough to see that what was on it was inedible. But I didn't know the Korchnois well enough to simply refuse. I took one spoonful and choked it down. I knew a second spoonful would kill me.

An awkward scene followed. They tried to persuade me to eat, but I held my ground. Korchnoi ate his helping as if nothing were wrong, and we returned to the game. Not a smidgen remained of his former good mood. I tried to concentrate, but to no avail. I couldn't think and yet I had to make moves. I made one "natural" move, a second, and then the advantage melted away as if it had never been there. It was a good thing I got hold of myself, didn't force the game, or try to prove something. Draw. In the days to come he never once succeeded in luring me back into the kitchen.

You can imagine how angry I became with myself, giving away victory in a short match without a fight. In the next game I didn't have to urge myself on. Korchnoi ordered the French Opening, then the Sicilian—it didn't make any difference to us how we played. I was now leading by two points. One more time, I'm thinking, I'll sting him and then there will be no way for him to play himself out of it. I had become terribly insolent. Some tricks, though, never worked on Korchnoi—he quickly evened the score. Then I came to my senses. He saw that now I wouldn't surrender to him so easily. Even though it was only a practice match, there was still the urge to win. To have an additional chance, he proposed, "Let me play White in the last game." His house, his rules. "As you wish," I said, but I vowed: Now that it's a matter of principle, I won't lose for anything. "But that's not my whole request," said Korchnoi. "I would like us to play a certain variation," and he named it.

You could say he backed me up against a wall, but I

was so angry I didn't care what we played. I stood my ground. The overall score was three to three.

After the match we both had mixed feelings. Victory had been only one move away and each of us had hoped to get there. But we didn't lose and that lessened the disappointment, especially for me, since I had just become a grand master, and here I had played to a draw with the challenger to the World Championship. Korchnoi also profited from this match. Making corrections in his preparations, he destroyed Geller, virtually dispossessing him of a single chance in their match.

That's how we were—our relations would become aggravated if I surpassed Korchnoi in something, and then they'd return to normal. I wouldn't call them friendly but they were definitely civilized.

We often met with mutual friends and played bridge together. Even in bridge he was aggressive, although he clearly didn't know the particulars of this game. Sometimes we prepared together for competitions and at other times we even took vacations together. I'll never forget the scorching-hot summer of 1972 we spent together in Dubna, outside Moscow, examining the games of the match between Spassky and Fischer, while around us peat bogs burned and haze floated in the off-white sky. Only after midnight we would walk down to the river and skinny-dip in the still-hot water.

His wife had a tempering effect on him. Next to her, he softened. He attempted to read books she thrust at him; he accompanied her to the theater and concerts. But over a book, or in the theater or at the cinema, he couldn't conceal his boredom. His thoughts were occupied by something else. Korchnoi seems to be driven by two things: "people are out to get me" and "where can

I scrape up some extra cash?" I remember how Korchnoi ran from his guests on his birthday for a brief appearance on television, for which he was paid pennies. It wasn't just for the sake of flashing momentarily on the screen. This was something he did on a regular basis in Leningrad.

Korchnoi didn't try to hide how he was, and this was hard on those around him. Yet he could afford just about anything he wanted, and he created his own enemies. That was something he really had a knack for.

Korchnoi and I were preparing together for the Interzonal Tournament in Leningrad when one day some guests showed up unexpectedly. It was a nice, pleasant evening and someone suggested we try to predict who would play in the finals of the candidates' match. When the final pair was determined, we would get together again and open up our ballots.

I remember I wrote *Spassky-Petrosian* on mine, certain they were the strongest candidates. Naturally, my selection also reflected my awe and respect for their huge talent. I didn't write my own name, for I believed that my cycle had not yet arrived. I had practically no experience at such a level and I considered the main opponents to be stronger.

Of course, everyone immediately forgot about those little scraps of paper. I did, too. But when the final pair was determined, Korchnoi and I, someone who had taken the ballots suddenly appeared and showed them to everyone. Only on one was *Korchnoi-Karpov* written, and I recognized the handwriting as Korchnoi's.

We didn't convene our former company because it had now become impossible. When I played the last game of my match with Spassky and it was clear I was a finalist, Korchnoi, who had made the finals somewhat earlier, went around in the press center and the spectators' hall and said to all our mutual friends one and the same thing: "You will have to choose between me and Karpov." It would be impossible to concoct a more foolish ultimatum than this. All of these people valued their friendships with both of us. It never occurred to any of them to uproot that over some momentary whim. Later it became clear that Korchnoi was not joking, and these poor people had to make a choice between us—Korchnoi wouldn't have it any other way.

But I've gotten ahead of myself, forgetting all that Furman did to help me in this match with Korchnoi. Many times I've thanked my lucky stars that I had the good fortune to meet him and work with him. I wonder if he hadn't died in 1978 how my matches with Kasparov would have turned out. Without a doubt they would have been different. Because, thanks to Furman, I would have been different. I would most certainly have continued to grow and develop with each year. I remember how after my matches with Polugayevsky, Spassky, and Korchnoi I felt renewed, as if everything was for the first time, everything was fresh and I wanted to play again and again. Now the feeling has become commonplace, everything is familiar and everything—thoughts, situations, and conversations—is old news. Furman's death killed something in me. I've become hardened and can't relax enough to let in something new and make it my own. The absence of novelty leads to boredom, and because of this I can't make myself work the way Furman and I once did together. Only a new task makes you look for new creative moves. But to renew yourself just for the sake of renewal . . . I don't think it works like that. Even a philosopher, who supposedly seeks the truth just for the sake of truth alone, actually pursues truth because it's in response to some genuine existential discomfort. All this leads me to wonder if, when a truly new and worthy task presents itself, I will be able to recognize it. More than ten years have passed since Furman's death and chess just isn't the same.

Furman lived with his wife on the outskirts of Leningrad in a small two-room apartment. About ninety-seven square feet, plus another sixteen square feet for the kitchen. It's not even worth adding in the foyer: it was so small that a normal-sized closet took up half of it, meaning that to leave the apartment you had to turn sideways. The smaller room served as their bedroom. In the larger room, about sixty-five square feet, were a sitting-room, bookshelves, a workplace, and a huge aquarium illuminated from below. Their son also slept in this room.

A few miles farther, beyond a gray field, was a gigantic pig farm, and when the wind blew from that direction, it was impossible to breathe. Shutting the windows had no effect—the stench seeped in everywhere.

I would get on the bus near my building and ride it to the last stop, near to where Furman lived. We spent many wonderful hours in his sitting-room at his polished folding table. Furman's chess set was excellent: a sturdy board with heavy, firm pieces, corresponding in form to the international standard.

We were alike in many ways, both easily excited. I preferred process to result, and he loved both the process of playing and the process of thought formation. Finally, each of us in his own way was well grounded in fundamentals. The only difference was that analysis predominated in me, whereas synthesis held sway for him. In general, we not only understood each other at a glance or in a word, but felt each other like our own selves. Thus, we worked freely together.

When I say that synthesis prevailed with Furman, I have in mind his imagistic perception of the world. Furman almost never got away from the image. Perhaps he didn't want to, although it's possible that he couldn't.

This explains, incidentally, one riddle associated with him. It's known that during my games in the candidate matches Furman guessed the overwhelming majority of my moves, so my thinking and level of play were clear and accessible to him. So what was his problem? Play yourself at this same level, I thought, move the way you guess, conduct yourself at the board as if you're filling my role, and your successes will become commensurate with the play and success of the world champion.

But when Furman took his place at the board, he couldn't do it. He couldn't imitate me, even though he probably wanted to. Like a child, he was so happy with any of his successes. For this alone he loved to participate in the same tournaments I did. Playing alongside me, he either charged himself from me or guided himself by my playing, as by a certain standard, but even for me it became difficult to compete with him. All he had to do for certain failure was to go to a tournament without me.

The reason, I think, is that when Furman guessed my

moves, each of them was for him a logical, natural building block, a part of the overall image. An absence of
responsibility freed him from his thoughts, and allowed
him to rise to his true stature. When he played alone,
the mandatory analysis and obligatory reckoning of variations destroyed the image; responsibility, the need to
make decisions on his own, destroyed freedom, and then
Furman's play was still correct and strong, but essentially
trite.

When I speak of my analytic streak, this should also
not be taken literally as a breaking up or division into
building blocks. I understand analysis as a process of
finding that essential truth which, given a chance to
develop, will create wholeness.

I'll explain this with an example.

I think I already mentioned that games—any games—
come easily to me. Not easy in the sense that I easily learn
the rules of a game. This is something almost anyone can
do. In saying "I learn how to play," I mean how to play
a winning game, a game with constant superiority.

The point is that most people think of a game only in
terms of participation and observance of the rules. The
former is passive, and the latter obedient. Maybe it's possible to win accidentally that way, or by beating the same
types of people. But if, among the players, there is at
least one true player, all the victories will come to him.
Why? Because a true player, getting to know a game for
the first time, deconstructs it down to its nuts and bolts
and learns the whole internal mechanism in the very first
tries. When he begins to play for real, he is capable of
extracting the maximum from any situation that might
arise in the game. His partners only observe the rules,

but he is guided by *principles* which are intrinsic to the game. These are the internal laws by which the game lives.

So when I say that Furman was a player, I mean his receptivity to the game, his ability to be engrossed in it and excited by it. Without this the game lacks a specific tone and emotional ardor, and is incapable of igniting all around it.

But Furman wasn't a true player guided by principles. He got his principles ready-made from people like me. A principle acquired secondhand loses its most important trait: individuality. Even though it's the same game for everyone, every true player has his own principles of the game that correspond to his taste, temperament, inclinations, and personality. These principles help him to express himself in a game. Individual principles of a game are like blood vessels uniting player and game in a single body.

For the ten years that we worked together, we used to play a card game called Siamese Fools for fun. And all ten years I beat Furman mercilessly, because I had created a theory for this game. Furman knew about this, but vanity did not allow him to ask out-and-out questions about it. Sometimes, though, he would inquire why I played a certain way and not another, and then I revealed to him the corresponding principle. Furman immediately added it to his arsenal and the next time he didn't understand my game, he would ask again. I didn't deceive or dissemble, but laid everything out as it was. I was certain that it would not influence the outcome of the game. Toward the end he complained, "What is this? Supposedly I already know everything that you know, and you still beat me."

I observed a long time ago that the public, for some reason, is convinced that a chess coach is smarter, more responsible, better understands chess theory, and is better acquainted with its practice than a sportsman. He only plays worse than his ward, although, according to the logic of things, possessing so many qualities, he should prevail in the game. The public considers the coach to be the mainspring in this working duet. As we like to say: Wherever the neck goes, the head will follow. All this is far from the truth.

First of all, a coach is a desirable, but by no means a mandatory, figure. Of course, you can't put a price on a good coach, but in the final analysis a chess player is capable of preparing on his own. No matter how important this preparation is (depending upon the strengths of the player himself), 80 percent of success is decided in direct combat with an opponent (if you don't take into account something that has become fashionable in our time, the home analysis, drawn out right to the victorious finale). The first great chess players, including the world champion, got by perfectly well without constant coaches.

Second, responsibility for the outcome of a chess duel resides with the player. He carries all this weight himself. But if he loses, then he can blame the coach for advising him poorly. In my opinion, this is improper. Any coach can overlook something or make a mistake, but what was the player looking at? After all, he is not a marionette. In victory, all honor goes to him and only his personality determines whether he will share it with his coach and how magnanimous he will be in his gestures. And only he gets the bitter praise of the vanquished. No one today remembers Botvinnik's or Petrosian's coaches, yet any chess fan knows that Botvinnik ceded his crown to Petrosian, and Petrosian to Spassky.

Chess is trial by responsibility. This is why many talented chess players who knew everything there was to know about chess were never outstanding players: The need to make a responsible decision at the board crushed them. They're like a donkey between two bales of hay who couldn't make a choice and died of hunger. I think that a coach is a frustrated player who participates in big games which would normally be inaccessible to him. He places responsibility on his player. That's why Furman guessed my moves. Not only did he know me and was himself a good player, but—and this is the most important thing—he was freed from decision.

It is characteristic of coaches to exaggerate their importance, at least before the public. They try to capture center stage. A player has to approach this with understanding. A person doesn't live by bread alone and applause is only for a few moments. The rest of the year the coach toils no less than the player, and sometimes much more. He rightly seeks the recognition, even if it is fleeting, for this labor. Of course, Furman was human like everyone else and, to some extent, this was true of him as well, but to a very small degree, and infrequently, like a light cold or fever suffered by a healthy child in the midst of an overall epidemic. He had different values, and these gave him immunity.

Our relationship was very close—he treated me like a son, and I saw him as my second father. We didn't simply sympathize with each other, we loved each other. But it was a common goal that united us.

We never once discussed the division of roles. Since Furman was so much older, wiser, and experienced than

I, I conferred upon him the right to be the voice of decision. But life quickly rearranged our places. Furman was not really suited for the first role; he wasn't prepared for such responsibility. Decision making, for him, was accompanied by physical torment. Unusually brave in everyday life, he lost this wonderful quality in a chess milieu. We never once talked about the casting of roles in our duet. Why bother? I think it was precisely to avoid such an unpleasant, and even humiliating—as far as he was concerned—conversation, he readily and thankfully accepted it.

He knew himself that he wasn't cut out to be a leader. A leader is purposeful. It doesn't cost him any effort to sweep away everything incidental. He takes energy from his goal and therefore is constantly directed to it, like a compass needle pointing north. He selects the most economical route and the most economical regime, because only this allows him to reach his goal in the quickest way possible.

Furman dissipated his energies in different directions. Without this his philosophy of life would not have worked, and without this he could not have derived satisfaction from life. For example, Furman developed a tremendous enthusiasm for bridge, coinciding with the beginning of our full-time collaboration. Enthusiasm is actually an understatement and does not at all convey the real truth. This was a disease of the worst sort. At first I didn't pay it much heed, since we were all players and all venturesome. I figured the flame would burn out, and it would pass. But Furman's enthusiasm quickly grew into a passion and passions do not bend to control—they enslave.

This was a late love, with all the things intrinsic to a

late love, like haste, blindness, and imprudence. Furman could play for hours, and he did. I know of one case in which he played forty-two hours straight. The other partners from time to time spelled one another and got up to eat or sleep, but Furman didn't leave the table. It's hard to believe, but it happened. All the other participants and eyewitnesses of this unique record are still alive.

As with other games, he didn't play bridge very happily. For this reason, there still exists in the chess world a popular saying: Victory is wherever Sema (Furman) is. Well, first of all, that wasn't said in regard to chess, as everyone now assumes, and not even concerning cards. In fact, it was uttered during a game of dominoes. Secondly, it was laced with irony.

It made absolutely no difference to Furman whether a game was played for money or not, although he preferred playing just for points. He and I were also alike in this respect. In our quest for the prize, we were more interested in the process than in the winnings themselves. When a player tells me that he plays only for money and can't play otherwise, then I have to think he doesn't love the game, that it's just a means for him.

Furman took to bridge just as completely as he did to chess. He bought books on bridge and studied the systems. He acquainted me with what he had read and understood, using me as his whetstone. In bridge, too, I had my own system of playing, formulated intuitively, and I have to say that for two decades now it has served me faithfully and truthfully, allowing me to be a worthy opponent even to professionals.

I haven't forgotten Furman's enthusiasm for bridge, because in the tournaments of those years it cost me points, sometimes important points. If a chess game doesn't end in the allotted time and the adjourned position is a difficult one, then you have to be able to rely on your coach. He's not tired, his mind is fresh, and he has experience which, in the analysis of adjourned positions, comes first. Finally, his detached view is so important.

I remember a game with Vladimir Savon that was decisive for both of us, for the national championship in Leningrad. I laid down a tremendous assault and at one point had a chance to win, but Savon sensed the danger and deflected it. Still, the game was adjourned heavily in my favor. Furman took the text of the game and went home to work on it. At dinner Tal and I exchanged opinions on strategy. But I was too exhausted to sit a few more hours at the board when I knew that my coach had already taken this burden upon himself.

In the morning Furman appeared with a completely different plan. I believed him almost blindly. Everything was in order, so I didn't bother to check it. When the game was resumed, such a hole opened up in his plan that I barely escaped, barely crawled to a draw. I began to look for the explanation as to how Semyon Abramovich could think up such nonsense. And then suddenly, by chance, I found out that he killed the whole evening at bridge and only at the last moment threw down the first thing that popped into his head.

This episode repeated itself at the Alekhine Memorial. In Leningrad it cost me the championship. True, in the future this never happened again. I told him, "Semyon Abramovich, you have to make a choice between bridge and chess." I was already first fiddle, and I had the right to demand this from him. Naturally, he chose chess.

What a coach's nocturnal "analyses" are like is best explained by a story Petrosian loved to tell. It was in the 1950's. Petrosian adjourned a game in a position known as the Queen's Endgame. It was a very important game for his ranking in the tournament. One look at his position was enough to know that its continuation would be rocky. A tired Petrosian asked his coach, Liliental, to examine the position closely, and went off to bed. In the morning he discovered a note under his door that read: "Dear Boy! There are a lot of bagatelles in the Queen's Endgame. Tigranchik, don't miss them!"

Whatever the case, Furman and I got used to each other, our work advanced, and it was visible in the results. Playing in all the best tournaments, I invariably ended up among the winners. Victory in the Leningrad Interzonal, which I shared with Korchnoi, was difficult and tortuous, but it gave me a great deal of sporting and creative satisfaction. Even though I had hoped to win the tournament, I couldn't predict, much less guess, how I would feel while doing it. I fought furiously, blind to everything except my next opponent. I didn't think about what was just around the bend, and then suddenly the clanging of swords ceased and an unusual, distinctive kind of silence reigned. As if coming to my senses, I looked around and saw that I was standing very, very tall. Only yesterday I had still been down, far down, in the chess crowd, and today I was standing extremely close to the summit. I raised my head, and saw the summit was a hand's breadth away. Only three steps remained: quarterfinals, semifinals, and finals. And then . . . Fischer. The great and inscrutable Fischer.

Just three steps, but I knew how incredibly steep they

were and therefore didn't kid myself. The amount of strength I had would determine how high my ascent would be. I couldn't predict anything more.

In order to climb up the first rung, I had to beat Polugayevsky. He was a strong player, and he had succeeded so well in chess before our meeting that I understood if I approached this match like a battle of pieces on a black-and-white field, I had little chance of beating him. But it's *people* who play chess—meaning intuition, temperament, character, and will during a battle carry the same weight as knowledge, experience, and skill. I reckoned that my fighting qualities would at least equalize our chances.

In terms of pure chess ability I also intended to concede nothing to him. I was never a punching bag—just to withstand the blows was not enough. I hoped to hit him back, hard.

My task was simplified by the fact that Polugayevsky, notwithstanding all his chess strength, was a player of very limited range. You can almost always predict exactly what and how he will play. For example, he played the white pieces positionally, solidly, and profoundly. He religiously believed that the right to move first offered an opportunity to construct the game in such a way that the black pieces would be smothered and crushed by a constant, inexorable press. He reasoned that it was enough just to do everything by the book to deprive Black of having a chance at salvation.

When, however, Polugayevsky was given Black to play, he became a completely different person: abrupt, extravagant, and even desperate. For the longest time I couldn't figure out where this two-facedness came from or how to explain it. No matter what the circumstances are, a person evaluates them according to the same pattern, the same measure, that's instilled in him. He can't be one way today and different tomorrow. He's one and the same, but circumstances change, and he is compelled to react to them differently. You can't change the circumstances—you have to adapt yourself to them.

The solution turned out to be a simple one. It's actually quite surprising how it came to me right away: Polugayevsky was recklessly audacious with Black and rocked the boat with all his might, because he clearly saw what a hopeless situation it was to play against White in positional, correct chess. Believing in the inevitability of the asphyxiating squeeze of White's viselike grips, he was prepared to go against himself and his nature just to avoid these grips.

It was fear that made him bold. I decided he wouldn't be able to withstand the simplest thing—my demonstration of certainty in my own strength and success. My confidence, natural in any battle, should have put him off balance right away, put him on edge, and then it was only a question of how long his reserve of stability would hold out. It lasted him for three games.

The fourth game turned out to be crucial. Exhausted by the endless calculation and recalculation of variations and crushed by my imperturbability, Polugayevsky got himself into time trouble and not only squandered the huge advantage he had gained up to then, but also compromised his position. In the resumption of play he tried to save himself by choosing, if not the strongest, then certainly an unexpected plan, which Furman and I hadn't considered at all in our home analysis. He couldn't confuse me, though. I understood his intentions and won the skirmish. That still wasn't the end. Only in the next game did Polugayevsky break.

To play him using his variations was the same as walking through a minefield, but that's exactly how I constructed this match. When you lose on your own field, the pain is worse. The risk was huge, but I wasn't afraid to take it.

Again I ran up against Polugayevsky's home preparations, and such magnificent ones that as soon as he made his move, I knew it was over and there was no way for me to save the game. Finding myself at the point of no return, I couldn't even get worked up over the situation. It happened, the deed was done, and nothing could change it. So I became philosophical. Surrendering was out of the question. I'm a player, and as long as I have at least one chance, I'll fight, so let's see how he's going to pull this off, I thought. I relaxed, answered his moves easily, and, instead of sitting at the board, strolled around the stage and mumbled a little song that suddenly came into my head: "Everything floats away like smoke." Only yesterday I was up one point—and now I had nothing.

To be honest, this spectacle was not planned in advance. It just sort of happened. It was precisely that unfeigned tranquility that shocked Polugayevsky. He saw my terrible position on the board, but I was acting so calm and playing with such ease, I must have seen something that he hadn't. He was a pitiful sight to behold. Over and over he calculated and recalculated the variations, and couldn't understand how I could save myself. Of course he couldn't—he was looking for something that wasn't there.

The result was a draw, akin to a catastrophe.

Polugayevsky understood that he couldn't win a single position from me.

What was most surprising of all was that this didn't reflect at all in Polugayevsky's attitude toward me. On the contrary, the worse his affairs went, the more courteous and benevolent he became toward me. Never again did I ever discuss, with him or with anyone else, a game that had just been played so candidly and in such detail as I did with him. These analyses brought us very close together. One of the paradoxical results of the match is that it presented me with Polugayevsky's friendship. If only all matches would end that way.

Polugayevsky's wife was just as warm to me during the match as he was. Chess players aren't that surprised by a display of nobility at the board; for the majority of them it's natural. But for a wife to behave in the same way toward her husband's "enemy" . . . I've never again witnessed such a generous display.

The match with Spassky was one I hadn't even dreamt of playing. If I could measure myself against Polugayevsky, then Spassky was a weight the likes of which I'd never lifted before.

I always had a special regard for him. Tal was always very distant from me. I understood and valued Petrosian, but we were too different and we looked at and interpreted chess differently. Spassky was not my idol, but from the time I began to understand something about chess and distinguish among styles, I singled him out and guided myself by his game as my standard of modern chess. I liked everything about him, from his subtle understanding of positions and his skillful mastery of dynamics to an unusual sharpness of sight which enabled him to see the gears of a secret mechanism, visible only to him. It had always seemed to me, even when I didn't know him, that he was like me in character. I understood him and knew how he wanted to move.

When I began consciously working on myself and devising a universalism of the game, I did so mostly because Spassky's game was distinguished by universalism. The fact that I pulled for him during both matches in the World Championship with Petrosian says nothing. When he became world champion, I figured this was only fair.

His match with Fischer was still looming on the horizon, but I was already waiting, anticipating it like a fine meal. Fischer advanced like a steamroller, flattening everything in his path, but Spassky, who until recently had existed as if above chess, almost never playing in tournaments, was a wall that even a sudden hit-and-run couldn't knock down. In comparing his best playing against Fischer's, I didn't estimate it to be any lower.

But suddenly I was invited to Spassky's training camp for the match. This was an honor. True, my star was already rising swiftly, my name already stood for something, and I had my share of overtures, but everything was still new to me, and the prep kitchen for the match to determine the chess crown was like a sacrosanct altar to me. To be there and to peer into the mystery of mysteries was something that even as little as one year before I couldn't have imagined, and now Spassky was *inviting* me. I was getting ready to leave for a tournament in Holland (it was a year before when Spassky had me rudely bumped from the very same tournament—fate loves paired events), and I already knew there would be other tournaments, but when would I ever again have the chance to work on chess together with the world champion?

So I set off for Spassky's camp. Naturally, I wasn't allowed to even get close to any prep kitchen. I was there by chance and was potentially dangerous. Only on rare occasions was I invited to participate in some banal and nonobligatory analysis of a Fischer game. I watched in amazement how Spassky did nothing.

At breakfast, he would animatedly recount the latest tale from ancient Greek mythology, which he read before going to sleep at night. Next there was tennis, followed by something else, anything at all, just as long as it wasn't chess. At that time he promoted the "theory" of a clear head for chess. If the head is clear and strength is fresh, he'd say, then with his talent he could outplay anyone. This "theory" was concocted by his coach, Bondarevsky, in order to rationalize the world champion's pathological laziness. I consider myself to be an idler, too, but the dimensions of Spassky's laziness were astounding. The fact that their portfolio contained a victory in the match against Petrosian, sustained after such a "preparation," didn't convince me in the least. Giving Petrosian his due, I still couldn't understand how they could transfer the experience of battle with him to the upcoming match with Fischer. After all, not only were they different people, but Fischer heralded the arrival of a completely different type of chess. Wasn't this clear to them?

Toward the end of the camp, Spassky, wishing to check his form, decided to play several games with me. In the first game, he selected the Ruy Lopez. I played White and quickly gained a winning position. All I had to do was hold on to it for a little while longer, but, weary from the previous inactivity and irritated by how I was being treated, I decided to show off and embarked upon unnecessary tactical complexities. This gave Spassky a chance to display his customary resourcefulness. I should have regrouped in time, changed the arrangement, and played to at least hold on to what remained. But I already realized my lead was receding, and I overplayed and lost. Spassky liked this game. He decided that his form was superior and there was no reason to continue checking it. My participation in his final prematch training was virtually limited to this one game.

The finale to this came a little later. The boss of the chess laboratory at the USSR Sports Committee, grand master Alatortsev, recommended on behalf of the chairman that I be sent to the match in Reykjavík as a reserve because I was the most likely future challenger. I didn't make it to Reykjavík because the report was overturned by the following resolution: "In view of the absence of any outlook in the near future Karpov should not be sent."

Neither before nor after did I ever work at chess so diligently. Furman and I worked out an overall concept and psychological strategy. I sought out weak links in the armor and fencing artistry of my opponents. Tactics were devised for winning right *here,* for delivering the strongest blow right *here.*

For Furman, this work turned out to be the best medicine against bridge. It exorcised bridge, like an illness, from him, leaving a melancholy feeling in its wake, as after any passion.

I tried to forget my reverence for Spassky, and I tried not to think about his grandiosity. I told myself that I had a task before me, a very difficult, but common, one.

I had to recognize this commonness and believe in it so that my opponent would be cut down to size.

The material from the Spassky-Fischer match proved to be invaluable from both a chess and a psychological standpoint. Fischer possessed an algorithm for battle against Spassky. True, he drove a little hard in the first game when Spassky clearly began to dry out the game. As I see it, Spassky, fearing Fischer somewhat, and attempting to gain equilibrium and confidence, decided to show at once that, whenever he wanted to, he could always play White to a draw. Fischer became enraged and started to demonstrate the opposite, that he could always intensify a game, sacrifice a piece for an equal one, commit himself, and still win. For anyone else such a defeat would simply have been a lesson, but Fischer extracted from it a concrete advantage multiplied by ten: So, I fell into a pit? Then I'll confound my opponent even more, so that when he tries to seek me out in this abyss, his head will spin.

Then he failed to show up for the second game, presenting his opponent with another point. This was an ingenious move, a move designed specifically for Spassky, a move that demonstrated he had superlative knowledge of Spassky. Had Petrosian, for example, been in Spassky's place, he would have lapped it up and reveled in this free point. But Spassky the philosopher lost his balance. His center of gravity shifted, and right then all of Spassky's assets dropped in value. He needed a good ten games, alternately tortuous, helpless, and tragic, just to find himself, but by then it was too late to save the match.

I knew that I would never allow myself anything like that. My respect and esteem for Spassky precluded it. I believe that chess, by its very nature, is fair play. Therefore, I considered psychology to be only part of a pure chess battle. We prepared two surprises for Spassky: the Caro-Kann Defense for Black and the periodic transfer to 1 d4 for White. Both surprises worked. Spassky, plainly unable to adjust himself to me for the entire match, had to confront a very uncomfortable opening.

In our preparations and plans we gave special attention to the opening, which was out of character for me. But Spassky's neglect of opening subtleties gave me an opportunity to seize the initiative at once. Of course, there was also a danger in his amateurish openings: he could invent something right at the board that would never be found in any textbook. But I was prepared for this. The match was played, not to verify who had the better memory, but to see who better understood chess and was better governed by it. Of all the matches I've ever played, this one turned out to be the most improvisational, the most "playerly."

It began on an unhappy note for me with a loss. I came to the board ill, suffering from a cold and a high fever. My head felt as if it were filled with cotton balls, and I couldn't pull out a single worthy thought from behind all this wadding. I had been sick for days and if I had had more experience I wouldn't have come to the opening, thereby postponing the beginning of the match until a later date. However, the doctors promised to take care of the illness, and the sports officials talked me out of spoiling the opening. They argued that there would be so many people, so many officials, everything had been planned in advance—in short, they were afraid of unpleasantries and trouble for themselves. I acquiesced. I didn't feel any better on the day of the game, and when I called for a time-out I found out that it's possible to take one on any playing day except for the first. Such are the rules.

Spassky didn't need much time to dispense with me. As he rose to leave, I asked him to look at several moments from the game. "Excuse me, but I can't," said Boris Vasilievich. "I have an appointment with a friend, and time is pressing." He apparently had no doubts that I wouldn't last long and, accordingly, had made an appointment within the time allotted for playing.

This victory over me in the first game proved to be just as fateful as his victory in the first game against Fischer. Deciding that it was all clear between us, he calmed down and relaxed completely, and even when, two games later, I evened the score, he still didn't grasp what was happening and continued in a state of Olympian assurance of his own superiority and overall success. Only the sixth game worked him up. I saw it in him. He was already a different Spassky: deeply wounded, confused, and disbelieving of what was transpiring. In order to get a handle on things, he turned to me immediately following this sixth game and suggested we jointly analyze it. "Of course," I said. I couldn't turn him down. I even forgot my offense at his refusal of my similar offer. I excused it because I was already standing over him. He felt it, too, but he didn't want to admit it to himself just yet.

Many years later he told me, "I can't play with you because I don't understand the way you play or your train of thought." In order for him to understand this and admit it, it wasn't enough for him to lose the match. He needed years of mulling it over, years of observing my play, and numerous unsuccessful attempts at finding the key to it. Fortunately, this match didn't ruin our relationship. And I don't consider myself responsible for making this great fighter gradually withdraw from the chess elite. It wasn't I who broke him, but Fischer. What our battle would have been like if Fischer hadn't come first, I can only speculate.

CHAPTER FIVE

 AND NOW TO THE FINALS WITH KORCHNOI. Because I thought I knew Korchnoi much better than Spassky, I feared him less. When I was asked before the match to evaluate my chances, I would always answer the same: "The playing will show." But I was already thinking about Fischer.

At first my relationship with Korchnoi was fairly good. I knew about the ultimatum that he had delivered to our mutual friends. He distanced himself from me to such an extent that nothing remained from the warmth of our former relations. Now it was all strict officiousness, cold correctness, and, only if he felt that he was risking nothing, sarcasm. Naturally, in preparing himself for the battle, he tightened the string connecting us to the utmost, but when circumstances demanded something else, he immediately slackened it. Thus, in Nice, at the General Assembly of FIDE, the International Chess Federation, where the rules and regulations of the impending match for the World Championship (either Korchnoi or me versus Fischer) were to be confirmed, we agreed to present a united front and stand to the death against Fischer's three demands: (1) a match of unlimited dura-

tion; (2) play to ten wins; and (3) in the event of a nine-
to-nine score, victory is awarded to the reigning world
champion. Korchnoi, aware of his inarticulateness, asked
me to speak at the general assembly on his behalf as
well as my own, to set out and explain our position.
Incidentally, after the match in which I beat him, Korchnoi began saying that Fischer's demands were justified
and should be accepted. I think this was very unbecoming on his part. He wasn't asserting the truth, but was
simply trying to spite me and throw thorns in my path.

In the meantime, we conducted negotiations about our
own match through representatives. Korchnoi insisted
upon this. I don't think it was because he didn't trust
me; he merely wanted to maintain a line of active
confrontation.

The State Committee for Sports insisted that the match
be held in Moscow, but we asked that it be situated in
Leningrad. First of all, Korchnoi was a native
Leningrader and, second, I was also living there and,
although I perceived that the majority of fans would not
be on my side, I wanted to fight for the hearts of chess
fans in the city I had come to love. Furthermore,
Leningrad guaranteed conditions for holding the match
no worse than those offered in Moscow.

To be fair, at that time it wasn't difficult to come to
an agreement with Korchnoi. The only serious stumbling
block concerned the time for beginning the games.
Korchnoi wanted to begin at four o'clock, while I wanted
to start at five. Since we still had not agreed on the
location of the match, Korchnoi proposed a compromise:
the match would be played in Leningrad (he wanted this
very much, but I was still hesitating), but the games
would begin at five o'clock per my request. We agreed.

With this agreement in hand, I traveled to Moscow to see Pavlov, the chairman of the State Committee for Sports. Pavlov listened to me unenthusiastically. "You're too simple-hearted," he told me. "You take Korchnoi too much at his word, a word that's not worth anything. In Moscow we would guarantee that the match be conducted under equal conditions and without excesses. Finally, such a match is a great event for the whole country, but you're reducing it to a clarification of relations between Leningraders." I admitted he had a point but I couldn't back off: an agreement is an agreement. It was left to Pavlov to back it up with his consent.

I had just returned to my hotel when the phone rang. On the line was Korchnoi. We hadn't communicated at all for about two weeks, and now he had somehow found the telephone number where I was staying. "I already know," he said, "that you were with Pavlov and agreed to everything."

"Yes, everything's in order."

"Not completely. You see, I thought about it again, and I've decided that I can't begin the games at five o'clock. I can only play at four o'clock."

What a dirty trick—he had made a concession only to get everything.

"But we agreed—" I began, still not fully comprehending what was going on.

"And I thought it over," Korchnoi interrupted. "I can't begin at five, and that's all."

"Then our agreement doesn't exist!"

"You could say that."

That was the whole conversation.

I sat there stunned and then I headed out to see Pavlov. He heard me out. I thought he was going to get angry with all this nonsense, but he only laughed. "I warned you, Tolya. You can't be a good guy with Korchnoi. He only understands force."

"So what do we do now?"

"Very simple. We'll teach him a lesson. First, the match will be played in Moscow. Second, the games will begin at five o'clock. That's my final word."

By the way, Korchnoi's representative, his friend Professor Lavrov, to whom I was indebted for the happy move to Leningrad, refused to play the role of intermediary after this incident, which I could more than understand.

The relocation of the match to Moscow caused unexpected difficulties with the arrangements. It's no secret how much a chess player's successful performance depends upon the efforts of the sponsors and organizers. In the past, the Armed Forces Club players didn't want for anything. The Minister of Defense, Marshal Malinovsky, was obsessed with chess, and especially followed the successes of that club's chess players. He didn't refuse them anything. By the time of our match, though, Malinovsky was already gone, replaced by a new minister, Marshal Grechko, who preferred tennis to all other sports. He related to chess fairly well, but he wasn't interested in it. Since his aides knew this, our problems never made it to the minister's desk. Everything was resolved (if resolved at all) at a lower level. In any event, no one was interested in getting involved with me.

The trade unions had already fulfilled all of Korchnoi's desires, but I still had no idea how or where I would set up my team.

Fortunately, Pavlov turned out to be strong in memory

and firm in word. An official dacha was made available
to us in the village of Otradnoye. The conditions there
were Spartan, and the food aroused a lot of grumbling,
but I still have fond memories of this place. We were
surrounded by the nature of central Russia: high and
lush grass, birches and spruces, a dark pond, and a small,
glassy river. On the down side, mosquitoes harassed us,
and sometime in the middle of the night a squeaking
cricket took up residence in my room. Even this had a
meaning of its own, for I suspect that had it not been
for these importunate neighbors, I wouldn't have really
appreciated the charm of our dacha.

I had barely settled in when I had to get a move on
and take the match in hand.

The match got off to a good start; I immediately seized
the initiative, and in the second game I enjoyed an outstanding victory. Korchnoi showed up for the third game
as if nothing had happened and came charging at me like
a bull. All right, I thought, let's see what you'll be like
after a second blow. I dealt him his second loss in the
sixth game, and again he didn't falter. I could see from
his playing that he was in excellent form, and for the first
time I feared the match would be much more tenacious
than it had seemed after the first four games.

Here I have to mention the episode with Rudolf
Zagainov, the first in a series of parapsychological acts
instigated by Korchnoi. Zagainov was responsible for
Korchnoi's physical and psychological preparation, but
this psychologist pretended to an even more active role.
Evidently, he promised Korchnoi (and, perhaps, justifi-
ably) he would directly influence my thinking. I won't
take it upon myself to judge how successful he was in
this endeavor, but one thing I noticed from the very first

day is irrefutable. There was something suspect in his glance. Otherwise, how else could you explain that I noticed it and singled it out among all the others? After all, everyone in the hall was looking at me. I would look up to see dozens of faces fixed on me. Many were familiar, but still more weren't, betraying various degrees of attentiveness and interest, and running the whole gamut of emotions from rapture to hatred. I never pay much attention to this but this gaze was relentless.

Then I saw him and felt it again during the second game, and again during the third. I can't say that he seriously annoyed me, but there's no question he distracted me. After the game I asked Furman if he knew who this character was sitting in the loge, relentlessly following me with his eyes. Furman explained, adding that he didn't like Zagainov's behavior either.

I immediately understood the true meaning of this action (I had done a pretty good job of studying Korchnoi). It wasn't so much a question of Zagainov and his attempts to alter my subconscious—this was only the means. The end was something else. With all his outward aplomb, ostentatious strength, and demonstrative assurance, Korchnoi was always a rather unstable and doubting person. Naturally, his game suffered from this and his sporting results dropped. Now he had empirically arrived at the conclusion that he always needed some kind of edge—if not a real one, then at least one that he could believe in, one that could inspire him, and one that he could count on. Only then could the Korchnoi known to everyone—confident, forceful, and ambitious—come to life.

It was at this point I remembered something he had said long ago (now I find it hard to believe that he and

I actually worked together on chess) about the need to have some kind of obvious, real advantage over his opponent in order to feel confident. The thought "I play better" was not enough for Korchnoi. He had to possess something his opponent did not.

Zagainov didn't bother me. Let him look! I knew that I would quickly get used to his stare, but I didn't like his role in Korchnoi's consciousness. I had to think up something along the same lines to deprive Korchnoi of this trump card.

I explained the situation to Furman. It was clear to him we had to neutralize Zagainov, but we didn't know how. You see, Furman wasn't just a chess player; he couldn't do anything else but chess. Without it he was like a helpless child. But he told me, "Don't concern yourself with it. Play calmly. We'll figure out what to do with this parapsychologist."

Furman already knew whom to hand the assignment to: my physician for this match, Gershanovich. I don't know why Furman placed such great trust in Gershanovich. Maybe it was because of his grasp on things, his practical gumption, or because of the vast number of acquaintances he had in medical and quasi-medical circles. The main thing is that the choice was a good one.

"Nothing could be easier," said Gershanovich. "I have a friend from the Military Medical Academy, a Professor Zukhar, a Ph.D. in psychology, not to mention a captain of the first rank. Up until recently he worked with cosmonauts. I'll ask him to deal with our colleague here."

By the next game Zukhar was seated in the spectators' hall, and Zagainov was either hiding or had disappeared completely, but I never again felt his obtrusive presence.

*   *   *

Meanwhile the match was heading toward one goalpost. On the outside, this was barely perceptible. It looked as if the battle were being fought on equal terms, but at decisive moments I had managed to outpress and outplay Korchnoi, and, from my position of strength, I was slowly nearing victory. Korchnoi lost, but he didn't bend. He felt he was lacking in some microscopic thing, and he persistently looked for it, and along with it a last chance.

I'll never forget that thirteenth game. Korchnoi, with a colossal advantage, already saw and tasted victory. He was working furiously at the board, rocking back and forth, sweating. Somewhere, though, he rushed, or got overconfident, and for an instant he relaxed his grip. That was all I needed to slip out from under him. Draw. For me it was the same thing as a win, but for him it was worse than any loss.

Then the seventeenth game. Again it was advantage Korchnoi, who with every move was becoming more and more assured, and my defeat seemed more and more inevitable. But on this day inspiration came: My clever defense was close to a miracle. I dangled over the precipice, holding on by my fingertips but even so I concocted all sorts of new problems for my opponent, confusing his game and dragging him down. I got what I was after: fending off my imaginary threats, Korchnoi got into time trouble and lost. Just a few minutes before, the score should have stood at two to one, and instead it was now three to nothing.

And I decided that the matter was finished. Only this can explain my play in the next game. To the casual observer it might have seemed that a draw comes from a position of strength. Furthermore, trying to understand what I was doing, I calmed myself with the same interpretation. In fact it was different. I slackened my efforts, shifting from a regime of maximum mobilization to one of economy.

I decided that it was time to keep Fischer in mind, and to conserve both my strength and ideas for the battle with him.

Elementary mathematical computation confirmed the correctness of this stance. In eighteen games I hadn't lost once, winning three and drawing fifteen. All I had to do in the remaining six games was accumulate two points, and I would be crowned. Quietly, calmly, I would trudge my way to victory, and nothing could stop me.

My confidence turned to casualness. I thought I'd already won. All that was left was to go through the motions by playing out a few more games to a draw. Of course, it wouldn't hurt to nail Korchnoi one more time, if the opportunity presented itself. I had already developed a pattern of winning candidate matches ahead of schedule and I didn't want to break with tradition.

In the meantime it was enough to put myself in my opponent's place, at least for an instant, for this concept to fall apart. Korchnoi saw everything in a different light. He believed that it wasn't the level of play that was beating him, but only chance that had propelled me ahead. He sensed that he only had to concentrate more, apply a little more pressure, and he would be on top. Only three games! And then the real playing would begin.

In the nineteenth game I stepped on a mine of my own making, and was destroyed right on the spot. This win animated Korchnoi, but while I was distressed by the loss, I reminded myself he hadn't outplayed me—it

was just an unfortunate accident. Next time I would just
have to look under my feet a little more closely.

Having drawn the next game, I showed up for the
twenty-first without a care, only to be crushed by a blitz-
krieg. I could have resigned with a clear conscience by
the nineteenth move, but I needed a few more moves to
see more clearly what was happening. In my opinion, I
spent almost forty minutes, no more, on this miniature.

This game had a background which deserves telling.
As always in such matches, each of the opponents, in
addition to his official assistants, has still other unofficial
consultants who help, some out of feelings of friendship,
others for idealistic reasons, and still others to settle old
scores, using your hands, with their offenders. Among
those with good intentions, Botvinnik and Petrosian
occupied a special place. Botvinnik sympathized with me
and supported the version of my studies with him. During the course of the match he would occasionally call
me if he thought it important to offer some advice to
me.

Petrosian's feelings were much more complex. There's
no need to speak of any sympathy on his part toward me.
What wasn't wasn't, but on the other hand he detested
Korchnoi and this was enough for him to come over to
my camp.

This enmity was mutual, went back a long way, and
was as old as their rivalry itself, a period spanning two
decades.

Petrosian developed earlier and had greater fortune,
for a time even becoming world champion. But
Korchnoi, the eternal challenger, considered himself no
less Petrosian's equal.

There's no need here to get into the lengthy and complicated history of their hostility, which at times has bordered on the ridiculous. I'll relate only the latest episodes. At the candidates' matches in 1971 their paths crossed again. It was already clear that whoever won would have to face Fischer, who was swiftly ascending to the chess throne. There was practically no doubt that Spassky would deal with him, but our sports committee decided that it was better to stop him on his march. Petrosian and Korchnoi were summoned and bluntly asked which of them had the greater chance against Fischer. Korchnoi replied that in the "Fischer age" almost no one had a chance, but Petrosian said that he believed in himself. At that Korchnoi was asked to throw the match to Petrosian, in compensation for which he would be sent to the three biggest international tournaments (for a Soviet chess player at that time this was a regal present).

No documents exist to substantiate this plot. But the mediocrity of Korchnoi's play and the fact that, considering his bitter nature, after he lost to Petrosian he remained on good terms with him implies that Korchnoi let Petrosian win.

But the idyll could not last long. Petrosian had a notorious appetite, and he didn't want to depart from his habits here. Korchnoi knew Fischer well, and in general knew a great deal, so why not make use of this knowledge in the match with Fischer?

This incident is known to me from Korchnoi's own account, although it generally received wide publicity in the chess world. After hearing out the request, Korchnoi could not contain himself and burst out laughing. "Now how the hell can I be Petrosian's second if it makes me sick to watch how he plays?"

That was the end of it. This wasn't just an explosion,

but a challenge, and Petrosian vowed to annihilate Korchnoi. And now he was trying to do it with my hands.

I have to credit Petrosian's intuition. His sense of danger was phenomenal. After the fifth game, a completely favorable one, he said to me, "There's something I don't like in the variation you played. I can't put my finger on what it is exactly, but I feel something is wrong there. You should have your coaches go over it with a fine-tooth comb, and it wouldn't hurt for you to take another look."

It was good advice, but I never got around to using it. During a match you do only what is absolutely necessary, pressing, and urgent. In our analysis, Black's position looked promising, even with exclamation marks.

Korchnoi would never have ventured it a second time if it hadn't been for one thing: The two British chess theorists, R. Keene and W. Hartston, arrived to lend him a hand. They told him that Karpov played a defective variation in the fifth game.

When I began to unfurl this opening again, I remembered Petrosian's warning, but now it was too late to go back. How could I reexamine the position with the clock ticking? I walked right into danger, telling myself that when Korchnoi showed me what he's got then I'd figure it out.

You can already guess what happened. When I finally saw the danger, there was nowhere to turn, and it was too late to retreat. The trap was slammed shut.

This was a cruel defeat. I couldn't for the life of me remember whether or not I had told Furman about Petrosian's advice to dig into the variation again.

Furman met me in a dejected mood. He didn't know

the whole scoop, or the background to this defeat. "Semyon Abramovich, something's out of whack with our analysis."

"It can't be!"

Of course it can—I remember the page from the notebook and how it was written down, and the green circles marking the moves that lead directly to this continuation. I still see it, clear as day.

And practically right after I'd pronounced these words, Petrosian burst in. He was enraged. You might have thought he lost the game. "Sema!" he shouted from the doorway, breaking into a stream of the bluest invective. "How the hell could you let this happen? I warned you: No way you can play this variation! No way! No way!"

Only three games before this I had been leading by a score of three to nothing, the match practically won. Only a few small technical difficulties remained, and already I was looking ahead. Three games, which still had to be played, seemed to me an endless minefield. What was the matter with me? I had no reason to fear games in which I played White. I felt confident playing White, but Black was another matter. You could be entrusted with White only if you were full of strength and confidence. Three games ago I was imbued with it, but not now, not now. . . . Still, in those moments when I could objectively evaluate the circumstances, I knew that wasn't so terrible. It was enough to be collected, precise, and technical. It was enough to tune up for tough professional play, and everything else would follow. But I had to play one game as Black and so far I couldn't imagine how I'd get through it. And if I couldn't overcome it, it was back to square one. I had to think up a plan for surviving this twenty-third game and then my strength and composure would return.

That is precisely the danger of such a contest: Once it approaches, it's difficult to get out of it on your own. To do so requires time, distance, and relaxation. You have to give yourself up to the process, as to a whirlpool. But I didn't have time. Not a single day.

So I needed good advice. I called Botvinnik.

Prior to this I had called him once or twice throughout the whole match, but never from any special need. Now I had to leave my pride at home. I needed help, and I wasn't hiding it. My playing had come untracked and I couldn't figure out why. Worst of all was that Korchnoi had pinned me with White, and I couldn't think of how to deflect his next attack.

"I'm not worried about you playing White," said Botvinnik. "Tomorrow you'll wake up in a different mood, you'll know what to do, and you'll calmly play your game. But first of all you have to know today what you're going to do in the next game, the twenty-third. And here I can give you a hint. Do you remember when Alekhine was playing Capablanca how he constructed an interesting position for which Capa simply couldn't find the right key?" Botvinnik named it, and I immediately remembered and understood what he was getting at.

"The idea is far from perfect," he continued, "but there are two indisputable points in its favor: it's nearly forgotten, and it's solid. With Black the position is a little worse, but you'll hold your ground against Korchnoi. The most important thing is that it will surprise him, and he won't be ready for it. He won't have any plans in place, he'll have to improvise something right at the board, and this will give you an edge. When Korchnoi realizes this, you can consider that you've slipped by him. Of course, you might not like the idea, but look at the game carefully all the same. If Alekhine played it, it means it can't be bad."

Furman and I looked at the game and, indeed, it really wasn't bad at all. I worked for a while on my position and went to bed calmer. I slept soundly, which is extremely important for me during a competition. In the morning I awoke cheerfully and knew right away how I was going to play this day. Approaching the twenty-third game calmly, I played well. Using Alekhine's idea, I quickly evened my position. Korchnoi was caught unawares by both my play and my change in mood. He became nervous, forced himself, and futilely tried to break the game. A draw stood on the board, but he didn't have the strength to take it away from me.

And in the final, twenty-fourth, game, I crushed him. There was a hole in his calculation, and as soon as both of us saw this, the game was decided. With each move I increased my advantage. Korchnoi's defeat was inevitable, and when he recognized this, he offered a draw. It's not in my nature to add insult to injury, so I agreed.

Even now I don't regret this, but sometimes I'm plagued by doubts. Maybe it would have been better to hammer the nail then and there. Maybe a score of four to two would have made Korchnoi more just in his self-evaluation. As it was, the next day he announced in an interview, "All the same I play better than Karpov." I couldn't, and still can't, understand what basis he had for making such a claim. Of course, he was magnificently prepared and fought excellently in several games, but in two-thirds of the games he sat in the front row and couldn't even lift his head. One of his victories was the result of home preparation, and another was simply a fluke. When it came to playing at the board, he never once outplayed me. Yet it seemed impossible for him to swallow his pride enough to give credit where credit was due.

Our relationship, broken at the time of my diplomatic battle with Fischer over the conditions for the World Championship, was partially restored after I was proclaimed world champion. Korchnoi sundered this relationship, doing everything he could to discredit me. As God is my witness, I responded only when it was no longer possible to hold my tongue. But he also took the first step toward reconciliation, volunteering to make a congratulatory speech at the celebration in Leningrad to honor my ascent to the World Championship.

Our war was over, and it wasn't difficult to keep the peace. Since I was living in Moscow at this time, our paths practically never crossed, but it was already too late to mend fences. I didn't feel any malice toward Korchnoi, but at the same time I felt no warmth either, and he, obviously, couldn't forget that I had shattered his dreams of a chess championship, and that sooner or later he would have to defeat me if he ever wanted to get into first place. And he wouldn't let it go. I suspect he never forgot about it, not for a day, and therefore always saw me as the main obstacle. Any other chess player in his place would have viewed me as just an opponent; for Korchnoi I was, and remained, the enemy.

At that time life was no bed of roses for him. Petrosian, who was dissatisfied with Korchnoi's loss in our match, thirsted for Korchnoi's blood and pursued him everywhere. Making use of his connections, he slandered him in the press and choked him through official channels. It was Petrosian who had the idea to disqualify Korchnoi and strip him of his grand master title. I categorically opposed this, and the venture came to a halt. A person can say any number of things in a fit of temper or in interviews to correspondents. You can censure him for this, but there was never any reason to doubt Korchnoi's professionalism. If a professional is deprived of his right to make a living by his craft, what's left to him then—begging?

Thanks to these efforts by Petrosian, Korchnoi was not allowed to travel anywhere for a long time. Our ridiculous system (mercifully vanishing with the advent of *perestroika*), in which you can't travel abroad freely and in which someone has to vouch for you (that is, sign a letter of recommendation written by you about yourself), provided the perfect opportunity to keep a person in the country with no grounds whatsoever. Some official has to sign your recommendation, but he doesn't know you and says he won't do it, or else he says, "I've heard so many bad things about you that I'm not going to put my career on the line."

All of Korchnoi's attempts to counter the vilification in the press and break through the bureaucratic blockade led nowhere. Petrosian had an all-out full-court press on him. Then Korchnoi turned to me for help.

I called Baturinsky and said, "I just saw the latest newspaper gibe at Korchnoi. It's time to put an end to this, since it's being maintained not so much on Korchnoi's old escapades as it is on the ambitions of his enemies."

"What are you talking about!" exclaimed Baturinsky.

Anatoly Karpov in front of a game demonstration
board, 1982.

Karpov and Viktor Korchnoi in Leningrad, 1974.

Boris Spassky and Nikolai Krogius on their way to the match with Tigran Petrosian, Moscow, 1969.

Chief arbiter Vladas Mikenas starts the clock at the 1984 match between Karpov and Gary Kasparov.

КАСПАРОВ КАРПОВ

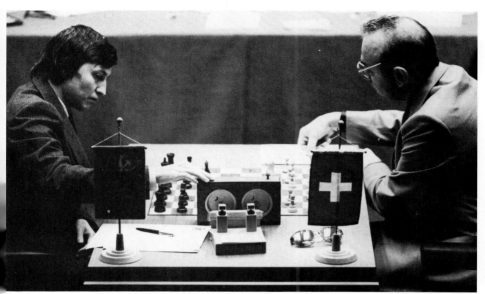

Karpov and Korchnoi struggling for the World Championship in the match at Merano, 1981.

Karpov and Kasparov at the 1982 Lucerne Chess Olympiad.

КАРПОВ   КАСПАРОВ

Kasparov looks on as
Karpov mulls over his next
move at the match in
Moscow, 1984.

Karpov's much-esteemed
coach, Semyon Abramovich
Furman, in 1977.

Igor Zaitsev and Karpov
experiment with new strategies
at a training camp in Latvia, 1983.

Karpov studies the board at a simultaneous exhibition of 700 players at the Hammer Center in Moscow, 1988. Thirty grandmasters competed, each playing twenty-five games.

As his father did before him, Karpov teachers his four-year-old son, Anatoly, the fundamentals of the game, 1983.

Karpov and his son, Anatoly, in their Moscow apartment, 1983.

Fishing in Latvia near the Daugava River, 1979.

Karpov shares a favorite meal at home with his sister, Larisa.

Cross-country skiing near Moscow, 1984.

Karpov confers with Boris Yeltsin at the Congress of People's Deputies, 1989. Karpov was appointed a member of the Moscow deputation that year.

Karpov with his wife, Natasha, in 1987.

Reflecting on the next move, 1984.

"Don't you know what will happen if we allow Korchnoi to lift his head?"

"I think, Viktor Davydovich," I said, "I have made myself clear. I'm against the continuation of this campaign." And I hung up.

Afterward Korchnoi turned to me again. No one wanted to sign his reference to travel abroad. I didn't have the right, yet the issue was not the signature, but the responsibility that a person took upon himself in doing so. And I gave my word for Korchnoi. As soon as the responsibility fell upon me, all the signatures appeared without a moment's hesitation.

Without question, this was a risky thing for me to do. I was convinced that sooner or later Korchnoi would end up in the West, but I hoped that he wouldn't do it just now, not under *my* guarantee. I don't think that such a turn of events threatened me with serious consequences, since there weren't any posts or positions which could be taken away from me, but it would have been unpleasant nonetheless—even very much so. He defected during his second trip, when my guarantee had already expired.

He used his first trip to the Hastings Tournament to take out his recordings and part of his library. During the second trip to the IBM Tournament in Holland, his evacuation continued. It should have been completed on his third or fourth trip, but here an unforeseen circumstance arose, connected with an event that shook the whole chess world.

The 1976 worldwide chess olympiad was coming up with Israel as the site. The teams from the Arab countries announced that they would not attend. The Soviet Union supported their boycott and a few socialist countries backed us up. A counter-olympiad in Libya was proposed, and our officials feverishly set to working this lode. There is only one way to interpret this: crude political intrigue, a primitive socialization of sports, and an attempt to create a schism within the chess movement for the sake of the careerist ambitions of select officials. Everyone saw and understood this, but then, still ten years before *glasnost,* one didn't call things by their true names. Then suddenly Korchnoi gave an interview. No one was forcing him, but since he was in Holland he decided that he could allow himself to be candid, and didn't hesitate to call a spade a spade. On the following day a representative of our embassy showed up at his hotel room and demanded, "Who gave you permission to say such things? Haven't you had enough unpleasantness already? Did you really think this would just be ignored?" Korchnoi, frightened that his right to travel abroad would again be rescinded, appeared at the Amsterdam police precinct and requested political asylum.

No doubt this was a stupid move. What would it have cost him to announce that he was remaining behind for creative reasons, as many of our artists had done before and after? Now his relationship with the state would be severed. Such acts in those years were classified in our country as betrayal of the motherland, a grave offense punishable, depending upon the political situation, to the *maximum* degree.

Knowing this, and warming it up with his usual persecution complex, convincing everyone (and most of all himself) that KGB agents were assigned to liquidate him, Korchnoi at first hid temporarily in the home of Ineke Bakker, secretary of FIDE, followed by other temporary hideouts in West Germany, and so on. His happy and free life abroad was in motion!

There are numerous people in the chess world whom I meet often and fight against at the chessboard, but who exert absolutely no influence on my life. We meet, but the contact between us is formal, fixed by a result or some kind of business matter. In either case it could be anybody, and nothing would change. But Korchnoi and I are fused in a certain and inexplicable way. This is manifested not only in the three grandiose matches for the World Championship, which became the main contest in both of our lives for ten years, but also by many other minor, striking coincidences known only to us, coincidences which can't be explained by anything save invisible threads joining our fates as one. I'll mention just one such coincidence. On July 25, 1970, at ten o'clock sharp in the morning, Korchnoi walked into the Amsterdam police station. Exactly at this moment, at seven o'clock in the evening at the other end of the world, I entered the Tokyo Hilton to see Robert Fischer.

Our second match took place at Baguio in the Philippines.

If someone had told Korchnoi or me half a year before that such a match would take place, both of us would have answered without thinking: Not a chance! This could only have been imagined in a nightmare. Such cities as Graz, Tilburg, and Hamburg had made bids for the right to hold the match. As far as Italy, France, and Switzerland were concerned, their conditions were significantly more modest and they had virtually no chance of hosting it. Baguio was also on the program, but only as an afterthought. It wasn't solid or serious, and only because of that we both began to develop this card, not so much because we wanted to win it, but to make it unpleasant for the opponent. I wanted Hamburg, Korchnoi preferred Graz, but we decided with the help of Baguio to fence with each other and drive each other to our chosen variants. Florencio Campomanes, president of FIDE, who had proposed Baguio, took advantage of this, and beat us both. If either Korchnoi or I had understood in time what was happening and what things were leading to, and if either one of us had yielded half a step, we never would have ended up in Baguio.

It's commonly accepted that a match begins long before the official opening. Right away, you start to do a psychological number on your opponent, demonstrate your confidence and strength, and choose the circumstances that are convenient for you but unpleasant for him. To concede even a little in anything is out of the question. What is normally valued in everyday life as wisdom is treated in this chess arena as a manifestation of weakness. It's not surprising that a third person would think to make use of this blind stubbornness. Instead of the usual, comfortable European cities, we had to play an interminably long match in distant, rainy, humid Baguio.

The story as to how we ended up there has become widely known. It is a graphically instructive lesson. One such incident, it would seem, would suffice to avoid a repetition of similar mistakes, but even as I write, everything is happening again: As I work on this book, a year remains until the next World Championship. FIDE chose Lyons, conveniently located, with wonderful conditions, as the site of the match, but there is one more candidate in remote New Zealand, virtually inaccessible for the press and fans. Kasparov has begun the game against

Campomanes in favor of New Zealand. Not because he wants to go there—of course not! It's simply the strongest card he holds in the psychological war before the match, and he intends to play it out as long as possible. The usual bluff. But then Korchnoi and I had bluffed with the candidacy of Baguio.

I had visited the Philippines before this, so I knew the place. I can't say that I succeeded in loving this country, but I like it very much. I was prepared for what I would see and feel in the Philippines, and my expectations were borne out precisely. As always in the tropics, the first day you're enraptured by the bountiful and colorful nature, but torpor quickly sets in and you quietly begin to fold up in your shell until only one thought remains: to get this thing over with as soon as possible.

I shouldn't complain, for we were treated well. We had excellent rooms in the Terrace Plaza Hotel, a spacious villa, with a panoramic view. There was a downside, though, unavoidable in the tropics. Dampness penetrated everywhere and into everything, and there was no escaping it. If you stopped wearing an article of clothing, in several days it would be covered by a thin layer of mold. For some reason I didn't bother to look in one of my suitcases for about ten days and, in the meantime, some minute organisms had managed to set up house in it. In the corners of the suitcase there were actually mushrooms growing. In inclement weather, which was practically always (we arrived in time for the typhoon season), you could see the swirling edge of a cloud creep down the hall of our open villa. Like a living creature, this thin cloud would leisurely float around the entire room, as if paying its respects, and then, suddenly, steal away.

*   *   *

Each match has its own face. Each has some feature which distinguishes it, making it unique and unforgettable. The match in Baguio was the most troublesome and most scandalous competition of all the ones I have ever been a part of. Fortunately, my opponent almost never succeeded in drawing me into the squabbles which he tried to provoke. Most of the time I tried to act like a detached observer, which only incited him further. I must have been driving him crazy with my cold-bloodedness. Sometimes, though, he got to me, and as the match dragged on, it happened more frequently. The monotony of the unvaried days was even more tiring than the games, and then I hit an unlucky streak which weakened my defenses even more. Against my will, I began to take each of my opponent's unjustified attacks personally.

Incidentally, "unluckiness" is too simple an explanation to be true. It was more likely a streak of physical and mental fatigue along with a feeling of impending doom. My sturdy, almost completed building of victory suddenly crumbled. Fortunately I managed to collect myself at the very last minute.

Korchnoi had created an atmosphere of scandal long before the first game. I'm not going to explain this by just his bad character. I'd known Korchnoi pretty well for a long time. I knew that he was capable of being cordial and tolerable, but I also knew that he possessed the willpower to always keep himself in check and control his actions. We had maintained civil relations for years prior to this match. But now we had a war, and what a war! It's important to remember that in *all* the matches Korchnoi played—and he played in a good many—scandal was intrinsic to the mood of the match. Korchnoi purposefully created a fistfight atmosphere in order to keep me from relaxing, so that, with one glance at Korchnoi, I would begin to shake. In the process, Korchnoi became outwardly agitated but inwardly he remained calm and focused on the game.

I take my hat off to him: Everything was excellently planned. Korchnoi only accelerated the vehicle of psychological pressure, but once the match started, he handed the wheel over to his girlfriend, Petra Leeuwerik. (His wife remained behind when he defected; he later divorced her and married Petra.) This woman raised such a ruckus that the journalists forgot about chess—the extracurricular circus was much more interesting.

Even before the opening, the itinerary of the match was strewn with thorns. In his prematch interviews Korchnoi would say anything to upset my equilibrium. Conversation between us was forbidden, and was carried on only through the chief arbiter. Finally, he decided to wear "mirror" glasses to "defend himself" from my "hypnotic" influence. Chess, the essence of which is communication and mutual understanding among people, was turned into a battleground by Korchnoi. Neither before nor after have I ever seen anything like it. I hope that fate will deliver me from such shenanigans in the future.

The match began somewhat slowly. We scrutinized each other, and felt each other out to see who was in what form. It was too early to lay out our trump cards, because our match was the first since 1927, to be unlimited in the number of games leading to six wins. To predict its length seemed impossible. The preceding match, in which I'd won an average of one game in eight, could not serve as a model here. There the goal had been to score more out of twenty-four games, and for the final third of the match I was concerned with only one thing: how to preserve my advantage. As it developed over the course of the battle, this was an errant strategy, and I paid dearly for it. This time the conditions were completely different, meaning a different level of play. I had no idea how it would unfold. I knew one thing, and that was I shouldn't rush. The battle itself would show the manner in which to proceed.

The first game—draw; second game—draw; third game—draw. The fighting was slow and cautious. It was not as interesting to chess players as it was to psychologists. In the second game, Korchnoi played Black, but I outplayed him. In the third game for the first time he used the Nimzo-Indian Defense and again he came up empty-handed. We agreed to a draw, with me one pawn up. I saw that Korchnoi hadn't expected such a beginning. He loves initiative, force, and pressure, but here he had to fight for equal footing. In addition, I succeeded in giving the impression that I had outplayed him easily, and this really made him angry.

The fourth game opened with a variation of the Ruy Lopez which I thought should have been Korchnoi's main weapon of defense in this match. On the fourteenth move he applied a continuation of it, which he himself had rejected in the first volume of the Yugoslav *Encyclopedia of Chess Openings*. Again I figured out what he was up to, and again we had a draw.

So far I was keeping my own cards close to my chest. I had to draw myself into the game, feel the pieces and myself in them. I wanted my ploys to be part of a full-blooded, integral game and not something separate from it.

Another reason I was slow in my shift to attack was that I first had to adapt to Korchnoi's psychological pressure in order for the external factors not to influence the quality of play. This pressure, which literally began the first minute of the first game, was very resourceful, assumed the most diverse forms, and continued virtually without interruption. Korchnoi carried it onto the stage, while his psychologists and extrasensory specialists worked it in the spectators' hall, and Petra Leeuwerik did her thing in the press center. My friends tried to protect me from her tricks and her inexhaustible absurd protests. These cheap tricks were simply a source of amusement to me, but it was still not an easy thing to adjust to Korchnoi's behavior. I'm not just talking about his mirror glasses (it's not enough that in and of themselves they're an unpleasant sight on a person you see for hours at a time in front of you, but when I was pondering a move, Korchnoi also turned his head so that the reflection from his glasses crawled along the board or pierced my eyes). After making a move, he would abruptly jump up, sometimes purposefully stand behind my back, readjust the pieces, spasmodically twitch his hands, or do anything else he could think of to distract me from chess and upset my balance.

The fifth game also ended in a draw. This protracted fifth game was adjourned three times. I began it unsuccessfully by losing a pawn. My home analysis contained holes, and at the board I committed inexcusable mistakes. Either God was on my side or else Korchnoi, blinded by the victory near at hand, lacked sufficient precision and stamina—I slipped out of checkmate and found an escape in what appeared to be a hopeless endgame. When Korchnoi realized this and saw that his victory had melted away like a mirage, he flew into a rage and, just to annoy me, played the game out to stalemate. Of course, that was his right. When you play chess in the courtyard, at the beach, or in friendly company, it's nothing more than an amusing diversion, but in serious chess a game is never drawn out to stalemate. This is part of the gentlemen's code of chess. But in this game, even when it was clear to all the *spectators* that a draw was on the board, Korchnoi obstinately continued to play until he could announce stalemate with a gloating look. Unable to win, he resolved, at the very least, to humiliate, offend, and unbalance me. To me, though, he was just pitiful, and the grandmasters who were in attendance at the match unanimously condemned him. There are unwritten rules which cannot be breached without punishment.

No one is insulated from mistakes. A mistake is not always the result of stupidity. It can show up, for example, as payment for risk or beauty (at the expense of simplicity), or as the result of ill health, when it is objectively beyond your power to alter complex circumstances. In any case, it's cause for self-knowledge and reason to take a sober and unbiased look at yourself, to make an adjustment in your actions and perhaps in the way you look at yourself.

I never made a tragedy out of mistakes, nor did I attempt to blame them on others. I have always considered the readiness to pay for something I've done, whether good or bad, to be one of the most important indicators of character.

That was exactly my attitude toward the way I played in the fifth game. As the saying goes, every cloud has a silver lining. I knew that the wait-and-see tactics against Korchnoi were disastrous, and that theoretically he was very well prepared, but physically and psychologically far from his best. Thus, if I were to stop playing conservatively, and sharply increase the richness of each move, plus bear the weight of the battle to the final hours of play, Korchnoi might not be able to handle the stress. Then it would only depend upon me to take advantage of the mistakes he was certain to make.

There's nothing unusual about this. I didn't doubt that Korchnoi would also extract some lessons from the painfully instructive fifth game. But I was wrong. Korchnoi's disappointment was evidently so great that negative emotions overrode his reasoning. It wasn't difficult to imagine him back at the hotel, replaying the game in his head over and over, move by move, not comprehending how he could have made such a weak move here, or not taken advantage of my negligence there. Such an appraisal is not only fruitless, but also harmful because it distorts the true magnitude of the event without allowing for a correct evaluation of oneself or one's opponent. It's one thing to conduct your analysis in quiet surroundings, but another thing entirely to replay the game. During a game the tremendous burden of all possibilities weighs upon you, along with the passage of time. Therefore we play at full strength only in those rare moments when, consumed by the process of the battle, we merge with the game to such a degree that everything else ceases to exist. That's why the psychological preparation is so important, for it relieves the player of the extracurricular chess onus. Korchnoi, whose practical experience is vast, knew this as much as I did. All he had to do was recall similar episodes from his practice and everything would have immediately fallen into place. Apparently, his emotions got the better of him.

On the eve of the match, the question of my psychologist, Professor Zukhar, came up. I don't know who first thought of this, but the notion of Zukhar's negative effect on Korchnoi was taken up in my opponent's camp with incredible fervor. The most amazing thing is that Korchnoi sincerely subscribed to it and thereby created additional difficulties for himself. Now, during a game, he couldn't help wondering if his thought processes were being tampered with or not.

Zukhar wasn't part of my group, but he arrived as a member of the Soviet delegation because I was counting on him. A chess victory is the result of numerous factors, not least of which are psychological. I always understood this and tried to take it into account, but it often came out differently from the way I wanted. Nevertheless, in chess the most important thing is chess itself and, when it gets hold of me, everything else fades away. In the meantime you have to look after your physical condition and the condition of your opponent so as to correct your actions quickly in case external circumstances begin to influence your play. It was precisely for this that I depended on Zukhar, on his advice and prompting, in case I overlooked something as a result of being engrossed in chess.

I also needed Zukhar. The match was going to be a long one. No matter how well I prepared, sooner or later fatigue would inevitably catch up with me. I don't know how it acts upon others, but at the first signs of fatigue I begin to have trouble sleeping; if I'm overfatigued, I can't sleep at all. This has happened on more than one occasion. Zukhar, quite conveniently, was a sleep specialist who wasn't tied down to a job and was ready to help.

In order to gather material, a psychologist has to observe. Zukhar chose a seat from which he could see both Korchnoi and me equally well, and he sat there without ever getting up. He took his role very seriously. And then someone decided that he was telepathically interfering with Korchnoi.

I understand my adversaries. If Zukhar didn't exist, then they would have had to invent him. If they had already hit upon the idea of announcing a protest concerning the yogurt which was brought to me during a game (I almost never drink coffee), then Zukhar was a gold mine.

For journalists and fans alike, two or three consecutive draws, regardless of their substance, are boring. What they're after are wins or losses; rarely is someone interested in the *quality* of the games. A point is something that everyone knows, even if they're only familiar with chess by hearsay. And when there are no victories, then any scandal at all seems exciting.

Petra Leeuwerik led the attack from the outset on all fronts, bombarding the organizers, jury, and judges with one official announcement after another. She demanded that Zukhar either be removed from the hall completely or seated further back, practically in the gallery, even though she had no grounds for this, something the officials patiently explained to her over and over. She presented her case to the journalists in vivid and dramatic tones. Finally, Korchnoi planted his people in the hall next to Zukhar and tried to distract him with conversations, or by walking by and "accidentally" bumping him.

But he understood that the blows directed against him would ricochet against me, and deftly he parried them, carrying his cross with patience and bravery.

The sixth game—draw; seventh game—draw. Korchnoi responded to Zukhar's presence by running from the stage as soon as he made a move. True, by the end of the games running was about the last thing he wanted to do. He had to sit at the board, without getting up. It didn't help, and finally victory came. This was a difficult victory in which I used an old home preparation. Korchnoi meditated for about forty minutes. I have to say that, having encountered something unexpected in the opening, he didn't look for the strongest continuation, but one which he didn't think we could have already prepared for. After forty minutes he made a move which we hadn't foreseen.

I spent the first fifteen minutes trying to recover from this psychological hit. Then I calmed down. All the same, my position was better. I could sacrifice a pawn, a move which had great prospects. I thought about it and made the sacrifice. Korchnoi took it. Then I began pressing him until the game ended in a clean checkmate on the board. And again a fuss was made—Karpov didn't win; Korchnoi lost because of Zukhar!

Victory brought satisfaction. After all, I had managed to do well. But it still did not relieve the tension that was growing inside me with each passing day. I couldn't rid myself of a sense of imbalance. Victory is fine, but there were still five more to go, and if each one was going to take eight games to accomplish . . . I had to break open the play more decisively, but so far I wasn't ready for it.

In the tenth game it worked. In an open variation of

the Ruy Lopez I employed a novelty connected with the sacrifice of a piece at 11 Ng5! Journalists ascribed its authorship to Mikhail Tal, but fairness demands that its rightful author be named: my second, Igor Zaitsev. Korchnoi endured this devastating blow and defended himself brilliantly, but I had many other possibilities at my disposal. Still, it didn't work out right away, and I resigned myself to abandoning my search for victory.

I should have called a time-out here, but I didn't think of it and instead concentrated on the game. I wasn't playing; I was just physically present on the stage. Supposedly I had done everything correctly and scientifically, but without energy or extra effort. Supposedly I saw everything, but selected only "strong" and "reliable" moves. When I saw the combinations I skirted them, feeling that I was in the wrong frame of mind to make them work. And then I collapsed entirely, absorbing one blow after another. I took them with a submissiveness so unlike me that, when I saw it was time to stop the clock, I was relieved that my torment at the board had ended.

The time-out which I did take after this brought no relief. If I had rested at the first signs of fatigue (the first is a loss of appetite for playing), then perhaps in two or three days I would have felt strong again. Rest didn't help, either. As I made my way to the next game, I lacked both excitement and the usual desire to play. Merely to tell myself that I had to pull myself together was not the way out. I understand that when an athlete gets ready to jump or to lift a weight it's for a one-time effort. But to get ready for a five-hour, taxing intellectual effort is another thing entirely. It's difficult to play chess, but it can be played well—easily and naturally—only when the moves are not wrung from you, but flow forth like music.

In short, I sat out the next game. If Korchnoi had understood the state I was in, it could have turned out badly for me. But I successfully imitated a desire to avenge myself immediately with an accumulation of confidence and pressure, while he thought only about how to contain me and even the score.

The danger was over but I knew this was only a respite. The crisis couldn't last forever. The tension had to reach the explosion point any second now. And then it would either be an ascension to new heights or the thankless task of picking up my shattered pieces.

The turning point came in the thirteenth game. I sat down at the board in one capacity, and rose from it in another. Moreover, I didn't feel the breaking point when it happened, but only afterward, in retrospect. Suddenly I understood that I was seeing everything around me differently: everything was bright and distinct and interesting, and suddenly I was very interested in the game's outcome, and I had no doubts that I would play at full strength in the next game.

It happened abruptly. Way to go, I praised myself, for having the courage to stick it out. Incidentally, Zukhar missed the onset of the crisis and was at a loss to explain it. He saw that something abnormal was happening and tried to penetrate my soul with the help of psychoanalysis, but I don't go in for this kind of thing and put a stop to it right away.

The thirteenth game began just like the others. I played without desire, as if the game were partitioned from me by glass. I did everything correctly, but I was always a little bit late. This eventually righted itself, but I still couldn't keep pace with my opponent's thoughts. Suddenly it was as if I woke up and saw everything from a different angle.

It was almost too late to correct the situation. I say *almost* because Korchnoi was already in time trouble. I decided to make use of this and to his surprise I broke the game, exposing my king and casting prudence to the wind. Korchnoi hadn't expected this. He lingered, while I used the slackening of his assault to my maximum advantage. Rapidly I began to crawl out from under him and I almost succeeded. The game was adjourned in a nasty position for me, but not one that couldn't be saved.

Both this spurt in the finish of the game and this optimism came from my new outlook, and Korchnoi was the first to feel it. He knew that he would have to resume the game against a *new* Karpov and he had to take into account not only the peculiarity of the position, but also my likely treatment of it. I became convinced from my analysis that I had chances to save myself, but nothing more than chances. But I had already looked a probable loss in the eye without fear. First, I thought, we'll fight a bit, and second, in the next game, I'll show him myself how the blow is delivered.

So I was ready for the most unpleasant resumption when Korchnoi suddenly called a time-out. It meant that so far he had not found a clear path to victory, and he most certainly wanted to. He convinced himself that the time-out was dictated by technical reasons, but I felt that something else was at play here. Uncertainty was getting to him and he was starting to give in.

The board on which we were going back and forth was sharply set into motion. I swooped upward, he fell downward. But for Korchnoi and me, nobody realized this.

I conducted the fourteenth game in my finest traditions. In the opening I employed a novelty; then, using the initiative obtained by it, my game became deliberate and precise. I took ground away from his pieces, leaving him to speculate when and where I'd strike and deliver the fatal blow. This game was also adjourned, but there were no doubts as to its outcome.

And now it came time to play them out. Okay, I thought, I'll lose one, win the other, but already the initiative is mine and I won't let it slip. Yet I saw the thirteenth game down to the finish in a fighting mood. As they said in the films I saw in childhood: Russians don't surrender!

I again counted on Korchnoi's time problems. I had a lot of time, and Korchnoi had very little, so I didn't rush. I decided to torture him for a little while. When the obvious moves were made, I stopped playing. I had, after all, a whole forty minutes compared to his one-and-a-half. I spent about ten of those forty minutes doing nothing but letting him suffer. Then I counted out a quarter hour. I had in mind an unassuming trap which I wasn't counting on too much, but I decided to lead my opponent to it; maybe in his haste he'd fall for the bluff. Korchnoi saw that I was planning something and bit into the board, as if he could devour it with his eyes. Then I advanced leisurely; he advanced instantly. Again I took my time; he didn't waste a second of his in response. I gave him the impression that I was attacking a pawn. He sensed something was wrong, but time was running out. He began twitching and defended the pawn with his queen. And right then and there the trap snapped shut: the queen was caught.

Instead of victory, a loss. Korchnoi was stunned. In only half an hour the fourteenth game was to be resumed—and the second consecutive loss. I thought that he wouldn't show up for this one, but he did, probably to show that he could accept the blows of fate. He even smiled. I can imagine how much this smile must have cost him.

Three to one.

What a sudden change from hunger to abundance! If you reason it out at the most basic level, then it follows that Korchnoi flinched and lost his balance, and all that had to be done now was press and finish him off. But there were two circumstances which had to be considered. First, the new situation in the match was also unexpected for me. I had to grow into it and master it. Second, it can't be forgotten that action equals counteraction. If the blows of fate topple some, then for others they temper, mobilize, and force them to act to the best of their abilities. Korchnoi was always one to rise to the occasion.

So I didn't force events, but continued to play as if nothing had happened, certain that the wave rising within me would sweep him away.

That's just what happened in the seventeenth game. Nothing in it hinted at its nature. Using the Nimzo-Indian Defense, I made a sacrifice, and my position became a little better as a result, but then I loitered and Korchnoi's position improved. I saw how be became animated, augmenting his advantage, surrounding my position, hitting ever harder, but I was so confident that I was practically indifferent to both his mood and actions. In such a state it's impossible to lose, because the essence of the game is revealed to you and you make flawless moves not because you have calculated everything precisely, but because you can't help but make such moves.

Again Korchnoi found himself in grave time trouble. I felt it was time to throw my pawns at his mercy, and with a small, mobile detachment comprised of two knights and a rook, supported by the king himself, I made a run straight for his king. This method, as old as the hills, is to strike with all the forces at hand at the right time and in the right place. He couldn't recover his wits and I slapped him with a beautiful checkmate using the two knights. One blocked the king while the other delivered the blow. So many chess players dream of realizing something like this on the board once in their lives, but to do it in a match for the World Championship . . .

How can I describe the second half of the match? If, after I had won and felt the strength and confidence increasing within me each day, someone had told me the match would last for another fifteen games and I would lose everything I had acquired, including both initiative and play, that even the score would eventually be tied and I would be one step away from losing the match, I would never have believed him. I couldn't have imagined that I would have to suffer through all this, not all at once, but stretched out over a period of so many terrible days. This is worthy of another book, one of deep and instructive psychological analysis. But I learned this lesson poorly. Six years later, playing my first match against Kasparov, I committed the same mistakes which I'm still paying for to this day. I will have to prove more than once my ability to take a hit. I'm ready for it. There's only one thing I dream about: that this test will be interesting to

me for as long as possible so that the day when I arise
and suddenly decide "The hell with it all, I'm fed up with
chess and I'm going to live like other people" will be as
long as possible in coming.

We took a break before continuing the second half of
the match. Korchnoi cut loose and began giving interviews left and right, each more scandalous than the last,
then he shot out of Baguio to Manila, where he accused
the organizers and me of the worst imaginable sins and
threatened to withdraw from the match. Naturally, I
didn't believe him. The prize money was a large sum,
but in order to claim it, even in the event of a loss,
Korchnoi had to play the match out to the end, or resign.
The second option was out of the question. Korchnoi
was a fighter. That can't be taken away from him.

   There was only one thing for me to do, and that was
wait. Typhoons strolled overhead in Baguio. This was a
period of intense boredom, with each day indistinguish-
able from the previous ones. I understood Korchnoi.
Seeing that I had found my game, he wanted to sit out
this streak and disrupt my rhythm. I became philosophical about it, as much as one can when one's best days
are being wasted. But irritation was slowly getting to me.

   Diplomatic contacts with Korchnoi's seconds didn't let
up for a single day and ended with a comical exchange:
Professor Zukhar for Korchnoi's mirror glasses. Two
thorns were ripped from the body of the match. What
else was there to do but get on with the games?

   Korchnoi reappeared with two soldiers from the Ananda
Marga sect, Stephen Dwyer and Victoria Shepard.

   I don't like deviltry, and to blame your failures on
black magic is, to me, simply vile. But so much talk

centered around these two terrorists, and so many times my losses were attributed to their parapsychological influence, that I simply can't pass over this episode in silence.

Judged objectively, the following two to three weeks I was in excellent form. I felt strong, I saw the chessboard well, I calculated the variations magnificently, and predicted my opponent's designs. I played the games confidently and solidly, leading them out to their inevitable denouements. At the very last moment, however, something inexplicable happened to me. I let my game slip. In a situation where I should have stopped, I continued to go forward; when I should have gathered my forces for the decisive blow, I made calm and "useful" moves; and I missed moves that any low-ranking player would have seen. Most offensive of all is that I began committing all these wonders at critical moments.

Nonetheless, there was no one to blame for such play but myself. I simply burned out from anticipation of the continuation of the match. I simply came to believe that, with such a balance in my favor and in such excellent form, all I had to do was execute technically for the match to end quickly. For the umpteenth time I experienced future victory prematurely, and I had nothing to complete it.

As far as Dwyer and Shepard were concerned, their presence was more important to Korchnoi than to me. I had assumed that a person like Korchnoi, with such a critical mind, couldn't take all this occultist stuff seriously. These two are like safety blankets for him, I thought. I'm not going to pay them any attention, and this will anger Korchnoi more than any of my other reactions.

A few years later I discovered it wasn't that simple. It turned out that the function of these skilled individuals was far from limited to their influence on me. Korchnoi had also prepared a psychological assignment for them. Here's a short eyewitness account by the well-known Swiss lawyer Alban Brodbek, who was Korchnoi's delegation leader in the next match:

> For the longest time I couldn't understand why a civilized person would have anything to do with some crooked shamans. I asked Korchnoi about this a number of times, but he tried to avoid straight answers. He dodged them and spoke in general terms like, Well, they help me with my confidence and stamina. But one time I walked into his apartment, not expecting to find anyone else there. I saw an amazing spectacle. There was Korchnoi, in an Eastern get-up, performing a ritual dance. In one hand he held a knife, in the other an orange which, as the participants of this act explained, represented Karpov's head. Korchnoi, after some steps and incantations, was supposed to pierce the orange. I was stunned and told Korchnoi exactly how I felt about this matter. But Shepard, who was directing the ritual, said that Korchnoi was affirming himself and accumulating spatial energy within.

I suspect that something like this had also happened in Baguio. But I didn't care about any of this. I felt strong. I would win, and the sooner the better. I believed I would manage to do so in another three to five games. Then, in the eighteenth game, when I had an advantage and should have won, I wound up instead with a draw. In the next game I held my ground, and in the twentieth I moved out ahead. Again I had the advantage, again I was pressing, and again I thought there was no way for victory to escape me. All I had to do was write down a normal move and victory would be mine, but instead I wrote down who the hell knows what, and—draw. Afterward, a famous law went into effect: If in a 100 percent situation you don't score a point, then a minute later in the counterattack a point will be scored against you. Suddenly I found myself losing.

My team was shaken, but I felt nothing more than mild annoyance. The score didn't mean anything. It was more important to make sure my confidence didn't abate. By the next game I set out for revenge. I could have sat awhile at home, thought up an excellent plan, and maybe I wouldn't even have to play it out, because Korchnoi had no chance for survival, or so I thought. But, instead, I wound myself up. He moved, I moved; he moved, I moved; he moved—in short, when I came to my senses, my hands were empty.

That's when I began losing sleep, and for the first time in the match, I turned to Zukhar for help. Losses don't torment as much as missed opportunities do. If I had played normally in the last few games, the match would have been over already. I couldn't understand what was happening to me. I analyzed each one of my actions as well as my thought processes, but I couldn't find any justification for what was going on. True, I still didn't doubt the outcome of the match, but I was working myself up into a frenzy. Somehow I had to distract myself, calmly prepare for the next game and go into it self-assured. But first and foremost, I needed to sleep, and I couldn't.

I agonized through half the night and then called Zukhar. He tried one thing after another, but to no avail. The next day I was like a zombie, and at night I didn't want to test fate. I asked Zukhar to try something right away. Again, nothing worked. "Forgive me," he said, "but it's beyond my power to be of any use to you. Your nervous system isn't yielding to mine, so if you want I can teach you my methods. But I can't put you to sleep." Pills were taboo for me. You can't play chess if you're groggy from pills.

And again we played to draws. Dwyer and Shepard disappeared from the scene. At the request of the judges and organizers they were forcefully removed not just from the hall but from the hotel as well. My friends reported this to me, hoping it would calm me down, but I waved them away in irritation. I knew that the problem was with me, and me only. I struggled with my thoughts and still couldn't understand why I could not exert my unquestionable playing superiority.

Finally I had a win in the twenty-seventh game. It couldn't have come at a better time. I'd already burned out by then, and somewhere in the middle of the game I felt completely drained. Korchnoi noticed this and confidently began his stride to victory, but he tried too hard. He wanted to win too much, and I was cold-blooded. I'd already used up everything I had in me, but I calmly calculated that my opponent's lunge would come right at the moment of his time trouble, and I therefore saved my last bit of strength for the final hour of the game. Everything was decided with several cool, precise moves.

One more step, one more win, and the match would be over. Yet I didn't know, couldn't imagine, didn't see at this moment how to make that final step.

The inadvertent victory, the one which I had walked toward for so long and had already lost hope of achieving, the victory which fell suddenly into my lap like a happy present, didn't fool me. Sure, I hoped that it would fulfill me to a certain degree, but this didn't happen and now a problem stood before me: how to play further? How did I fail to make use of such excellent form and so many wonderful chances? What then could I count on in my depleted state? Our camp was celebrating. Everyone was sick of Baguio and eager to leave, so I tried to isolate myself so as not to spoil their fine evening. No one could have helped me anyway. No one could have even hinted as to what I should do, or as to how I should continue.

I lost the next game, but I wasn't upset. Actually, I expected it. Then, because of a time-out, we had a weeklong break, but it didn't help me. When it came time to play again, I had nothing left to play with. Again a loss, the second in a row. Then I managed to break his momentum by fashioning a draw. Then I lost again. It seemed like ages since I was up by three games. Now the score was deadlocked at five to five, and no one could guarantee what tomorrow would bring.

What distinguishes a player from a nonplayer is that if a player loses consecutively, he doesn't crumble to pieces and give up. He continues to move forward, knowing that the losing streak will eventually end.

Korchnoi's camp was jubilant, and the press buried me. I was standing on the precipice, but unlike everyone else, I felt Korchnoi's time had passed and mine would soon come again. I had to wait just a bit longer to accumulate mass and momentum. So I decided to leave chess behind and spend a day in Manila. This was the idea of my friend, the cosmonaut Vitaly Sevastyanov. We drove 150 miles one way, met with friends, spent three hours cheering for our team in a basketball tournament, and then drove 150 miles back. Any other time, after such a trip, I'd be exhausted, but that night I felt as if I'd been doused with cold water. I showed up calm and confident for the thirty-second game. Korchnoi hardly looked at me, and he ceased to exist. If you see before you the same person week after week, then you can guess his mood and condition from one glance. Korchnoi understood even before I did that this game would be the last one. And I saw this in his fleeting, averted glance.

I executed this game in the way I wish I could always play: calmly, easily, without emotion. I saw the whole board, and I controlled the play from beginning to end. I immediately envisioned the strongest moves and checked them only afterward so that a stupid accident wouldn't disturb my march to victory. I didn't rush events, so the game was not completed in regulation time. But victory stood on the board. Back home we looked at it closely and concluded that Korchnoi had no chance for salvation. As a joke we announced a competition for a non-winning variation by White. I remembered how many "miracles" I'd created in this match, but felt that they were all in the past and, for the first time in weeks, I fell asleep almost as soon as my head hit the pillow.

I knew the game wouldn't be resumed. That's what happened. But Korchnoi lacked the character to end this match on a happy note. In a note to the chief arbiter he wrote that it was impossible for him to continue the match; instead of an honest resignation he had to leave the match unfinished and hand the matter over to the jurists who would attempt to play this empty card in later years.

I was sorry that Korchnoi showed such lack of spirit. I can understand that, during a match, in the heat of battle and in a state of agitation, a person sometimes doesn't see things clearly. But later, when everything is over, when the passions are left behind and you suddenly realize that this is nothing more than chess, a game which symbolizes wisdom and nobility, then you should stop all the fussing and honor chess for giving meaning to our lives. Our incredible battle deserved a beautiful and illustrious ending.

Incidentally, three years later, after losing yet another match to me in Merano, Italy, Korchnoi ended it with a note, written in his own hand, with the following message: "I hereby give notice that I am resigning without resumption of play in the eighteenth game and the whole match, and I congratulate Karpov and the entire Soviet delegation for their magnificent electronic technology. Korchnoi." It's not as if two machines had played, while he and I sat somewhere in the back, or behind the stage, and programmed them with moves and original plans. But if this is to happen, then thank God it's not for years to come. Besides, what difference does it make whether you consult a computer or a volume of the Yugoslav *Informator* in your preparation for a match?

Korchnoi was already a different person in Merano. His aplomb and spite were still there, but his strength had decreased. For a while he still clung to technique, experience, and preparation, which had always been his strong suit, and sometimes when he pulled himself together he squeezed out excellent games, but these were merely drops in the bucket. I understood this almost as soon as the match in Merano began. For ten years he had been my constant and threatening opponent, and suddenly I realized an era was ending. I won't hide the fact that at the time I was glad of this, but, as time passed, and I realized that Korchnoi would no longer try to overcome me, I felt that my life was emptier because of his departure. Just think about it! Only eight years ago I had thought there was no one else left near the top. Kasparov had already come upon the scene, patiently climbing and pushing his way through. I knew of him and I had watched him, but back then he seemed so small and unthreatening.

I remember Merano with fondness. It seemed to me impossible to improve on the nature, the people, and the organization of the match itself. Victory was unconditional and swift—six to two in eighteen games.

Evidently, Korchnoi also felt that his best days were behind him and bowed out during the next cycle—a London match against Kasparov. At first Korchnoi led both in scoring and playing, but in mid-match, he seemed to remember that his finesse would run out when he played me. It was as if he were replaced by a shadow of himself. I don't mean to judge him—anything can happen in chess. Some people say that he no longer wanted to take me on; others say that Kasparov got under his skin and broke him. Both hypotheses are possible, but there is one small detail that bothers me: Korchnoi always hated his match opponents, and if he lost to them, they were his lifetime enemies. But, in spite of the resounding defeat he suffered at Kasparov's hands, Korchnoi remained on good terms with him. And a precedent had already been set when he conceded to Petrosian the right to play against Fischer.

When there was nothing left to share with me, Korchnoi softened toward me. You might say that our relations normalized. We even played bridge together, but this didn't last for long. It was enough for our paths to cross in any competitive situation for his old charm to resurface.

In Brussels in 1987, I was challenging in a tournament and had to beat Korchnoi. It was my last chance for a top place. I put myself in a good frame of mind, but didn't betray it right away. I was playing Black. I waited for Korchnoi to reveal his game plan, and, when he showed me that he had already settled on a draw, I began to play more abruptly than usual.

Korchnoi didn't like this. My play caught him unawares, but he defended himself brilliantly and almost evened the position. He only had to make several precise moves to even things up. I saw the moves he needed to make, he saw them, and yet he still offered a draw. Had my situation in the tournament been otherwise, I would have accepted a draw. But I needed a win and told him to continue. Here the old Korchnoi appeared before my eyes. A grimace contorted his face. He reached for the pieces as if this game caused him the greatest disgust. But he made good and accurate moves, precisely those moves which would lead to a drawish position. I foresaw that in one more move I'd be surrounded, and there was nothing more to be squeezed out of the position. I made an obvious move, attacking Korchnoi's knight. Not looking at the board, nor removing his ironic glance from me, he reached for his king. I looked at the board and when I saw that the knight remained in combat, such obvious surprise was written on my face that Korchnoi froze. Realizing he had done something terrible, he gazed slowly along the board. For several minutes he looked in horror at the king he was holding in his hand and at the knight which stood in combat. Then suddenly

he slumped, reached for a form to sign, and just as suddenly tossed it aside, yelling that it wasn't for me, and
not with *him*, to play such drawish positions for victory.
He swept all the pieces from the board and ran from the
hall. Unfortunately for him, television recorded this game
from the first minute to the last, and everything he did
at the board was later shown to the whole world.

After this tournament, in which I eventually placed
third, Korchnoi vowed that he would never again sit
down to play with me, but he quickly forgot that vow.
And again it was business as usual, chess and bridge,
until the next incident. Upon his arrival at a tournament
in Linares, Spain, where I was also playing, and where
the chief arbiter was supposed to be my old friend and
advisor Baturinsky, Korchnoi announced on the day of
the first round that he would not play a tournament
where the arbiter was a "shadowy colonel." He was made
an offer: Baturinsky would judge all games except his.
Korchnoi would not agree to it, saying that in this tournament it was either Baturinsky or he. What is most
surprising is that he was supported by many grand masters, including Yusupov, Belyavsky, and Timman, who
justified himself by saying that if he had to make a choice,
then in the interests of chess he would take Korchnoi.

This roused my indignation. I told Jan, "I can understand the Soviet grandmasters. They're not wealthy or
independent. They can be bought. But you're a free person from a free country. You know that Baturinsky is
seventy-five years old, he's not in good health, but he has
tremendous experience and authority in the chess world.
He flew a great distance to be here not by his own initiative, but by invitation of the authorities. For what? To
hear undeserved insults? To suffer the cynicism of these

young people, for whom momentary profit is the most sacred thing? Are you really going to support this unconscionable action?"

To the organizer's credit, Korchnoi's undertaking was a total fiasco. He subsequently admitted that this was not an impulsive action but one that had been thought up in advance with Boris Gulko. But at the last minute Gulko "jumped ship." "I like this tournament a lot," he told Korchnoi. "If your action had gained the upper hand, I would have gladly supported you, but in this case, forgive me, I'm going to stay and play."

So Korchnoi left by himself.

CHAPTER SIX

MUCH OF MY LIFE HAS BEEN TAKEN UP with fighting Korchnoi, but that's not what my life is about. I worked very hard at chess, played in tournaments, made friends, traveled around the world, tried to arrange my daily life, tried to understand myself and others, and tried to find the source of altruism and the sources of deception. In airplanes and hotels around the world I have had a lot of time to think things over. I concluded that I see and feel everything much more keenly on a chessboard than in daily life, where many things—like death, betrayal, and perfidy—don't sit in my consciousness even though they are well known to me. I knew that I had to accept them as a given, but I couldn't do this. There are some things that are always painful. You can't get to them, nor can you adapt yourself to them.

Yet those three matches with Korchnoi were the major milestones of those years. I strode from match to match as from one peak to another. These peaks were strictly related to sports and, though they influenced other aspects of my life, for me these were merely trials. Life lay between them, and it was life, not trials, that mattered.

But winning has always been extraordinarily important to me. At any game I sit down to play I have only one goal: to win. Otherwise, why play? But winning just for winning's sake never drove me. For me the most important thing in a game is enjoyment of the game itself, from its flow, its process, its sudden reversals of fortune. To find the most precise path to victory; to find an elegant solution; to overcome the tremendous resistance of your opponent—these are the things worth playing for. And to win not only in separate games, but in matches for the World Championship.

I don't know how Fischer feels about it, but I consider it a huge loss that he and I never played our match. I felt like the child who has been promised a wonderful toy and has it offered to him but then, at the last moment, it's taken away. I can't speculate about the match's outcome, but I don't doubt for a second that it would have been the most memorable one of my life. It would have elevated me still higher as a chess player. No matter how tense and rich my matches with Korchnoi were, they were somehow not the real thing. Fischer was greater, and matching wits with him would have fully challenged me. It would have forced me to give absolutely everything I have and then, perhaps, I would have learned my true depth. I would have been able to judge what is in my powers and what is beyond them. All these years the feeling has stuck with me that I sometimes play at half-strength, sometimes at 80 percent, and rarely at 90. Even in matches against Korchnoi when I was on the edge, and even when I have yielded to Kasparov, I knew that I wasn't playing at my very best. I played according to the situation and the partner. With Fischer

I would have had to play a different kind of chess, and I still can't get over the fact that it didn't happen.

Naturally, I was happy when Max Euwe crowned me with the laurel wreath as world champion. Like any professional chess player, I had aspired to that dream for years. But that wreath was missing the most important leaves—the signs of battle with my brilliant predecessor. I tried to console myself by rationalizing that there are many things in life we don't see or experience, many things that pass us by, many things which we never even hear about. But this is weak consolation. I devoted my life to chess, and I had a chance to test myself at the very highest levels of my time, but this chance was taken away from me.

I first saw Fischer in 1972, soon after he became world champion, at a tournament in San Antonio. I was nothing more than a promising young grandmaster. The organizers asked Fischer to commemorate the tournament with his presence. He showed up on the final day, which wasn't the best thing that could have happened. The winners, myself included, calmly divided up points and Fischer, who sat in the audience for no more than fifteen minutes, realized what was going on and left. Prior to the opening of the tournament, which the organizers delayed to coincide with his appearance, he graciously met with all the participants. He and I hadn't been introduced before and he said a few polite words to me. I was struck by his gaze. He was not at all the way he looked in photographs. I didn't see any severity in him, but rather a sort of gentleness and patience. Incidentally, I never again saw that in him. I still remember his unique ursine gait. He walked awkwardly, his arms and legs not moving against each other as with other people, but together—simultaneously left and right—which resulted in his swinging from side to side.

America's response to Fischer's championship was amazingly fast. Prior to his victory, chess was certainly not one of America's major pastimes. When we traveled to the tournament in San Antonio, we discovered to our surprise that it was not such an easy thing to buy a chess set, let alone chess clocks, and hardly anyone had heard about chess literature. But by the end of the tournament that began to change. Soon after, I flew to America again and found the country in chess fever. Chess accessories were diverse and in abundance.

At this time I hadn't even dreamt of measuring myself against Fischer, but I had studied him and been fascinated by him. Even then I was struck by his single-mindedness. Fischer, while still in his youth, had made the world chess championship the goal of his life, and he pursued this goal with fanatical obsession.

I believe that Fischer surpassed all the former and currently living grand masters in the ability to produce and process chess ideas. He was of the old school; that is, he worked alone. It's an established fact that he didn't have any constant assistants and he didn't rely on others' ideas. This is what sets him apart from Kasparov, who comes equipped with the ideas of a huge entourage. I think Kasparov rarely uses these ideas "live" but they are raw material he adapts for his personal use.

Fischer was unique in his solitude. From an early age he learned to work independently, to comprehend the secrets of the openings, to prepare for tournaments and to study adjourned positions. Soviet chess journals presented him to their readers as a limited, uneducated upstart from Brooklyn. But in fact he knew several languages and had seen many things. He understood people, but as a philosopher he was weak, and this led to his downfall. Naturally he didn't like the Western or Soviet press. He believed that journalists who write about chess don't understand the essence of the game, or the meaning of a chess player's actions.

It seems to me that the reason for his tragic break with the chess world was the excessive demands he placed upon himself as the world champion. He believed that the world champion has no right to unsuccessful games, much less a defeat. Perhaps he went even further, not allowing himself to make even the slightest chess mistake. The solution to this stress was obvious—he stopped playing altogether. Fischer placed before himself a superhuman task and failed.

I understood that his was the only path to perfection and, as it turned out later, to chess perdition, but then it was still too early to talk about it, although I felt it was a very fine line. I tried to understand his logic and his goal. Any chess player in his place, who had just won four games in a row from Larsen, would have carried the match out to victory at a deliberate pace by drawing four or five games, or as many as necessary to win. But Fischer continued to fight in each game as if it were the first and only one, as if the whole match depended upon it. He never indulged himself or his opponent. This was Fischer at his finest.

Fischer's integrity was evident in any one of his actions. Even his shortcomings were inseparable from him; they were aspects of his integrity. That's why initiative in a game, a tournament, a match, and even in each separate episode was so important to him. Initiative provides the best means to be your own self, to preserve your integrity. And if Fischer was leading in a competition, if everything was developing naturally and logically, then he had no equals. If he immediately led in scoring, there was no stopping him. But it's not a question of statistics in his favor. For example, breaking his play in the first game of the match with Spassky, Fischer extracted huge psychological advantages from his loss and wasn't afraid to miss the next game, having correctly guessed that by doing so he would annihilate Spassky.

In the beginning of each competition, Fischer was wavering and uncertain. I think that the first round was always torture for him, and sometimes even the second and third rounds were as well—until he was convinced he was capable of his trademark superior game. For as long as this clarity and self-consciousness failed to arrive, for as long as he felt unsteady and uncertain, Fischer was nervous and highly unpredictable. It was this that made him quit many tournaments. It *wasn't* fear of his rivals, or an incomplete sense of himself as a player, or a lack of self-confidence. It was the uncertainty of his readiness to create exactly that style in which he sat down to play. Chess is indebted to Fischer for igniting interest in chess *worldwide*. The world—with the exception of a few countries, like the Soviet Union—was essentially indifferent to whether Spassky or Petrosian received the chess crown, or whether Tal or Keres, Bronstein or Korchnoi won in the Candidates Tournament. But when Fischer began his triumphant march to the chess summit, there was a sporting—and political—fascination to it: Who would come out on top—the lone Brooklynite or the united phalanx of the strongest Soviet grand masters? It was the favorite topic of the man in the street: one against all. This heated up interest to such a degree that for a time chess became the number one sport in the world.

Chess players are forever indebted to Fischer for improving the status and financial rewards of chess. Before Fischer even the best professional chess players in the West could barely make ends meet. Matters were a little better with our players because we always had the support of the state, such as it was. In 1971 the prize money for the quarterfinals Candidates Match between Geller and Korchnoi was 150 rubles (about $240.00 at the official exchange rate), with 90 percent of that going to the winner. Only three years later I was awarded *1,200* rubles for my victory against Polugayevsky in another quarterfinals match. By today's standards that's a laughable sum, but it was already much higher than in the previous cycle. For beating Spassky in the semifinals I got 1,500 rubles, and for victory over Korchnoi in the finals my share was 1,800 rubles. When the prize for the winner at the all-stars tournament in Moscow was announced at 2,000 rubles, the organizers figured they had practically gilded the participants. This was a real event for Soviet chess: the USSR Council of Ministers made a special decision and went out of their way to show the whole world we were nobody's fools. For comparison I should note that Robert Byrne, who lost in the quarterfinals to Spassky, received a bigger prize than I did for all three of my winning matches put together.

The next time I met Fischer, was in Japan. It was organized by Campomanes, who was to do everything he possibly could to arrange a match between us. He understood that this was the only possible way to keep Fischer competing and he felt a historic responsibility for prolonging the chess career of this great player. I can only imagine how deep Campomanes's disappointment was when he finally realized that all his tireless efforts had been in vain.

But in Tokyo it was still a long way to that. In Tokyo Fischer and I met for real. We took a good look at each other and sized each other up. From the outset I sensed his respect for me, and I treated him the same way. This wasn't difficult for me, since I always held him in high regard. I am glad that our meetings took place, and that we became close. I wish we had been able to play a match, but it just wasn't meant to be.

We didn't have to struggle for a topic of conversation, because there was only one: The match between us had to be played. I wanted it, Fischer wanted it, and, even though our views on the match's regulations were at first far apart, neither of us doubted that in the end we would find a reasonable compromise.

Fischer's obstinacy is well known. Spassky put up with a lot from him, and I had to be pretty insistent about a reasonable solution to our conflict. But now I was in an optimistic mood. There were no intermediaries between us, and I saw this as a guarantee of success.

Negotiating with Fischer was not an easy thing to do. Once he got something in his head, he stood his ground and wouldn't listen to his opponent's arguments. For our match, he wanted to play to ten victories in an unlimited number of games. In the event of a score of nine to nine, he would keep his title. When I heard this, I realized what a long road I still had to travel in our negotiations. Steeling myself, I began methodically explaining to him why this plan would be almost impossible to realize. If one of the players begins to win all the games consecutively and each week three games are played, then even in that best-case scenario the match would last a month. But if he wins one game in three, then already the match would go for about three months. Since both Fischer and I rarely lose, even that scenario was unlikely. Back then I couldn't imagine how it would be possible to play even three months in a row. Fischer didn't know how he'd do it either, but he still wouldn't back down. Then I suggested that after playing three months we have a fixed recess. He was unyielding: there would be no recess. Obviously he was afraid that all the Soviet grandmasters would tutor me during the break.

Yet no matter how difficult the first steps were, we were both enthusiastic and wanted to play our match. After the first meeting I was still hopeful, but I was beginning to have my doubts about Fischer. At the third meeting I saw from his very first glance that Fischer was burned out. Perhaps he was tired from thinking about this match and had been negotiating with me more from inertia than from a desire to realize his intentions.

After the talks we set out for a stroll around Tokyo. I was afraid that autograph hounds would harass us, but, to my amazement, not one person approached us. Here were two of the best chess players in modern times, whose photographs practically never left the front page, walking down the street—you'd think at least someone would have noticed. Later I understood that such a thing is possible in only one place on earth: Tokyo.

One photograph—the only one in which Fischer and I are together—was taken. The chairman of the Japanese Chess Federation, Matsumoto, ingratiated himself with

Fischer, who disliked journalists even more than their articles, and took our picture "for his family album." A few days later the shot was sold to Agence France-Presse, who in turn distributed it worldwide.

Up until then Fischer and I had managed to keep our plan a secret. I knew it would be impossible to keep this up for long and, in accordance with Soviet procedures of the time, I had to keep "the proper authorities" informed in order to obtain approval for both the negotiations and the match itself. But sports bureaucrats, whom I could approach right away, didn't decide such matters themselves; here the leaders of the party apparatus were needed, but I didn't succeed in getting through to any of them.

I was still looking for ways to get to them when suddenly this snapshot appeared. An immediate scandal ensued: Karpov, it was said, has entered into collusion with Fischer, and for an incredible sum has already sold the title of world champion.

What in fact happened was this: Fischer sent a telegram to the FIDE Congress in Nice in 1974 demanding that the number of games in the match be unlimited up to a total of ten wins. FIDE rejected all of Fischer's demands, but made a decision to do away with the limit of games and play to six wins.

Under pressure from the U.S. Chess Federation and its director, Edmund Edmondson, and with the active participation of Campomanes, a special session of the FIDE Congress was convened in February 1975 in Holland, where all of Fischer's demands were met, except for the one concerning a tie score of nine to nine. Fischer would not back down from his ultimatums and refused to play the match for the world championship under the auspices of FIDE.

I can understand the alarm of the sports officials, who had managed quite well without Fischer. They still remembered those difficult times when Fischer had threatened our grandmaster, when they were hard-pressed to explain all this "upstairs." With Fischer gone, everything was wonderful. Our officials could travel to rich foreign cities, live in luxury hotels, and cut their modest coupons from the successes of our grandmasters.

These were difficult days. I told myself how little the title of world chess champion meant in my country. I could be dressed down by the most insignificant chess clerk. One of them, Nikitin (the second of the future world champion Kasparov), even kept a dossier on me. For several months Nikitin tirelessly combed the foreign press, searching for any confirmations of the claims that I had sold off the integrity of Soviet chess.

No matter how tense the atmosphere was back home, it did not lessen my desire to play the match. And one month later I was back negotiating, this time in Cordova, Spain. I was there playing in a tournament, and Campomanes again made use of the occasion to bring Fischer over. Fischer sympathized with my problems and was glad I hadn't backed away from our plan. Our talks progressed only a little, but I wasn't worried about this. It's best not to rush such matters, since, after all, we were talking about the title for the best chess player in the world.

This meeting was significant—as we had done in Tokyo, we decided to go for a stroll along the streets. But within minutes we had to save ourselves by fleeing from fans throwing themselves at us. But Fischer's adventures didn't end with this. Somehow a journalist found out which train he was taking to Madrid and hunted him down. In Madrid he had to duck for cover in a private apartment.

After this meeting something stopped working in Campomanes's machinations. I pestered him as to when we would continue our work on the terms and conditions. Negotiations continued, but only through him. My final meeting with Fischer took place in Washington after an entire year had passed. Everything was prepared for it, the terms entered, and the conditions named. All that remained was to agree on some trivial details concerning the official title of the match and then to sign the copies of the agreement. Fischer insisted on calling it "The Match for the World Championship among Chess Professionals." I'll remind the reader that this was 1977, the height of stagnation and hypocrisy in my country. It would have been enough for our bureaucrats just to see the phrase *Chess Professionals* for them to come down on me. I would have been banned from playing such a match. I explained this to Fischer again and again; he replied that he understood my difficulties, but he couldn't compromise. Finally Campomanes managed to talk him into signing the agreement as drawn up, and then the official title would be decided later. Fischer would be presented with at least three new titles to choose from.

Reluctantly agreeing, Fischer took pen in hand. I was about to put my signature on the other copy, when I saw that Fischer had set his pen back down again.

"What's the matter, Bobby?" asked Campomanes.

"I can't do it like this," said Fischer. "I can't do it in parts. Either all at once, or nothing."

Something in him had changed. It's difficult for me to say what exactly, but something snapped and right then and there I realized that our match would never take place.

Many years have passed, but I am still asked the same question: How, in my opinion, do I compare with Fischer?

I consider this question to be ridiculous—a world champion's strength has to be assessed by his level of play in his best years. It has to be assessed only in comparison with those chess players against whom he played, and from among whom he ascended to the highest chess peak.

That's why I don't see an objective criterion for comparing my chess strengths to Fischer's, just as it's impossible to compare me with Capablanca or Lasker. Styles, yes. Styles can be compared as much as one likes. For this there's more than enough material. But not strength, because our rivals were different.

Fischer's strength can be evaluated only in comparison with the best chess players who surrounded him. And if we're talking about the Fischer of 1971–72, then it has to be admitted there was nobody who came close to him. He stood alone, and all the others, including Spassky, were somewhere below him.

It's a different matter with Kasparov and me. We can be compared indefinitely. He is the world champion, but the score in games played between us is virtually even; he leads by only three. At the match in Seville we played to a draw, and in the very first, in Moscow, Kasparov was barely visible, and if I had not then begun playing the fool, then perhaps this wouldn't be a topic of conversation now. By the way, Kasparov won the World Championship only in the very last game of our second match, in a game which, as analysis shows, I should have come out on top. But due to a bad habit of mine I committed a mistake and ruined a good game. And I lost everything. Wasn't everything decided in our last London-Leningrad match by literally one move?

In the spring of 1991 I played two games against Kasparov, in Spain and Holland. In Spain I had a slight lead, but Kasparov managed to pull out a draw. In Amsterdam, playing Black, I absolutely outplayed the champion, and in a moment when, according to the grandmaster Gennadi Sosonko, who was commenting on the game for the public, it would have been much more difficult to draw than to win, I relaxed and committed the most egregious error. The result was a draw. I speak of the New York–Lyons match later in this book.

Kasparov is proud of the fact that he managed to surpass not only Fischer's ELO rating (or his ranking among world chess players), but also the ultimate height of 2,800. I understand when journalists are amazed by this and trumpet it everywhere, and I understand the wonder and excitement of the fans. But I want to say that it is even more absurd to compare Fischer's chess strength with that of Kasparov, in whatever way, than it is to compare Fischer and me. How can you compare the different chess games and different opponents between then and now? Most important, the conditions for calculating ratings have changed. The fact is that any competition was calculated for Fischer, no matter what place he occupied in it, and whatever result he showed. In our time, though, the calibration is done a little differently. If you win a tournament or share victory with someone, but don't accumulate the necessary number of points according to your rating, your coefficient does not go down. In Fischer's time it would have. The first time, it means you have an advantage. What comes of it? Having won a tournament in Reykjavík, Kasparov—whose rating is slightly better than mine—should have dropped in his coefficient, but he retained his previous one. In sharing first place with me in a tournament in Sweden, Kasparov should have suffered terribly in his coefficient, because our result was very low, but here he got away with it. I did, too, because in this tournament, I also should have suffered a loss. I don't deny it: the rule by which a victor does not drop in his rating is logical, but unfair if we want the ELO coefficient to be an indicator of the true strength of a chess player relative to his contemporaries.

Each of us has contributed no small amount to chess. I am proud of my contribution, and Kasparov has already succeeded in doing a lot. But to be on an equal footing with Fischer—I don't know anyone else in the history of chess to whom we owe so much. Before he came along the popularity of chess was extremely limited, but Fischer made it a worldwide game. He elevated chess's popularity to such an unlikely height that, almost twenty years later, we are still expending the capital accumulated by him. No one from our generation of chess players, nor the one to follow, should ever forget that we are living off the dividends guaranteed us by Robert James Fischer.

It's hard to describe how I felt when I realized there would be no match with Fischer. It was a great loss. The first time my match with Fischer fell through, it was more annoyance than anything. I hardly knew him and

I judged him by his psychological attacks and illegitimate demands concerning the conditions of our match. This time, though, I had come to know Fischer well, we understood each other and I was quite taken with the idea of our match. I felt empty—there was no pain, only regret. I realized that what could have been the brightest event in my life was not going to happen.

At the same time I learned what true loss is. This can't be called a blow of fate, since I was prepared for it by its slow approach. But something died within me, too, some part of my soul became numb on that day when my best friend, my second father, Semyon Abramovich Furman, departed from my life.

I had never stopped to think about what he meant to me. He was simply intrinsic to my life. I became so accustomed to him that, even knowing and remembering about his lethal disease, I never once thought of how I would get along without him. And suddenly, he wasn't there. As I said, it wasn't a close friend that passed away, but a part of me, and now I would have to judge people for myself, make choices and decisions, do what he used to do for me so calmly and quietly.

There was still chess. I had my struggle, which to this day I can't imagine without Furman, but suddenly I understood I was on my own, one on one, against Korchnoi. There were still my chess-playing friends and my loyal assistants, but for all their competence and devotion they were a far cry from Furman. I knew nobody would ever replace him.

We buried him on a cold and rainy day in March. I flew in directly from Yugoslavia where I was playing a tournament in Bugojno. I didn't even try to hold back the tears. I looked at him for the last time, not consciously trying to remember anything from our shared past. Memories came unbidden, and only the bright and happy moments were recalled—that was how much Furman meant to me, that only with joy in my heart could I think of him.

Of course, I also remembered him otherwise: demanding of himself and strictly following doctor's orders in the first years after the operation, when no one knew how long he had to live. But when five years of abstinence had passed, Semyon Abramovich decided there was no longer any reason to live according to others' prescriptions.

The former ascetic turned into a lively, devil-may-care individual. He began to smoke more than he ever had in the past, allowed himself a shot of vodka, and often not just one. He stayed up late in endless conversations, in between twisting the dials of his radio so as not to miss his favorite commentator on the BBC, Aleksandr Goldberg. He was the life of any gathering. He never tried to stand out in a crowd, but his powerful charm attracted attention, although among people he usually preferred to keep silent.

And then, in autumn 1977, he suddenly took a turn for the worse. He didn't show it, and maybe he didn't even admit it to himself that his old ailments had returned. Probably there was no pain yet, only an inexplicable weakness. We were in training in Kislovodsk, and he had to fly to Belgrade for the Spassky-Korchnoi match to examine the playing in person and size up our opponent-to-be. He didn't want to do this; he didn't want to leave me. He still wasn't aware of what was happening, but his body knew everything, and the agony of the end close at hand spilled into him and governed his behavior.

Nevertheless he flew to Belgrade, and returned complaining the spicy local food didn't agree with him. He had sharp pains in his stomach. The doctors diagnosed appendicitis, and ordered an immediate operation, but Furman refused. "I'll let them cut me, but only in Leningrad." He flew out to Leningrad when he was diagnosed with cancer. It was too late to operate; the metastases had burst through like an explosion and struck him throughout. But he still hoped to live awhile. He understood that the path to Baguio was already forbidden him, but only death could liberate him from preparation for the match. He reflected on the dynamics of the development of Korchnoi's tastes, estimated where he would go and how to meet him there. In conversation with this hopeful and lively man it was impossible to imagine that he was in constant pain. It was said that he requested a pain-killing shot for the first time only two weeks before his death. Up to the final day he was a burden to no one. I remember how, on the eve of my departure for Yugoslavia, we sat on the windowsill, warming ourselves in the bright February sun, listening to the drip of thawing snow outside, and remembering our favorite old stories. I never saw him alive again.

Exactly a year later my father passed away. Again in March; again without me.

It's more than ten years already and I still can't rid myself of the thought that I was indirectly responsible for his death. The doctors assured me this was not the case, that cancer doesn't happen in a moment, but I remember that the disease exploded in his body in the days when I, having lost three games in a row to

Korchnoi, was on the edge. And although I know that I have millions of fans (and every day the mail brings dozens of letters), there was never another like him. He and I lived as one soul, and when I was feeling bad, I knew that he was feeling the same exact pain. I think this sympathetic pain struck my father down.

I say this because I understood him unusually clearly. I am indebted to him for everything that is good and everything that is best in me. For me one glance was always enough to know what was in his heart. It was also the same for him with me, I think.

It was in February, and again I had departed for a tournament, only this time to Germany. The doctors had reassured me that my father was still strong and would easily live until summer. But these words could not lift the weight from my soul. Instead I believed my father's eyes, in which I saw that the end was near.

But I told him we'd still fight awhile; and when he got better in the spring we would definitely take a trip to Zlatoust and visit our favorite places. He said yes, held up the conversation, led it around to my affairs, and laughed at my strained jokes.

On the last day before my departure he took a long walk, then his lunch was brought to him in an isolated area of the hospital. Later I saw how tired he was and I made him lie down. When he closed his eyes, his face became gray and drawn.

It was time to go. I told him: "Hang in there, Papa; I'll return soon, and then you'll see—you'll get better with the warm weather." He nodded, opening his eyes with difficulty, all the time holding my hand. Then he said, "Don't worry. I promise I'll hang on . . ." Only then did his fingers relax their grip on me.

In the doorway I turned around again. My father looked at me with large eyes. It was as if he wanted to absorb me into himself. I understood he was saying goodbye forever.

At the tournament I managed to play four games. Each day I thought of my father, but something suddenly grabbed onto my heart—and I finally resolved to call the doctors. It was on the evening of March the third. The physician on duty said, "He'll get better if you can fly right now to Leningrad." "What? Is his condition serious?" "No. But he'll be better if you return. . . ."

What did chess matter now? I explained my circumstances to the tournament organizers and said I was leaving. Unfortunately, the next day I was to play a game against Lyudek Pachman, and I knew for sure that he would make a dirty political show out of my exit. Even though he was warned, he showed up in the tournament hall and pointedly sat at the table until he got bored, and then he exclaimed to the journalists: "You see how the world champion treats a Czech dissident?" I couldn't have cared less. I tied up all the formalities in no time and took the first flight out, sped in a taxi from the airport straight to the hospital, but I was too late. When I saw the people crowding at the doors of his isolation compartment, I felt completely alone.

True, Mama was still alive, thank God, but her love for me prevents her from understanding me. We just can't be together. Yet I'm a family person, and it's essential that I have someone with me. Before it had been Furman, but when he died, his place in my life became empty. I didn't recognize this then; only afterward, analyzing the course of events. I understood later exactly what propelled me to do what I did. But then I simply decided that it was time to raise a family. So I married Irina Kuimova.

This was not a hasty marriage. I had known Irina for almost five years, and from year to year I became more and more convinced that she was the person with whom I could join my fate without apprehension.

The family of a chess professional is far from normal. Traveling constantly to tournaments, a chess player on average spends up to half a year away from home. For me it's an even greater amount of time. The family is constantly on edge from the stress the chess professional endures. When he plays—this is the maximum tension; when he prepares for a tournament, all his strength goes into chess; finally, when he suffers failure in a tournament, no matter how he controls himself, this affects the family tremendously. It's not surprising that not every wife wants to put up with this stress.

Western chess players often travel to tournaments with their wives. Organizers look calmly upon this, because it doesn't usually require any additional expenses. But our sports bureaucrats blocked this with all their might. There was no reason for this, but they wanted to exert their power, to emphasize in one more way that a chess player is nothing more than a helpless servant to them. Now this has changed and we have come up to Western standards, but ten years ago it was a period of "stagnation," when the bureaucrats would put even the world champion in the position of a servant. So for me every trip with my wife turned into a huge ordeal.

In observing other chess families, I was afraid the entire time that what looked at first glance like a solid marriage could at any moment crumble. As experience showed, my fears were correct. Early on I became materially independent, and even highly secure, by Soviet standards. Insofar as I constantly had to fend off the attacks by women hunting for a financially secure husband, I developed a wall to repel any thoughts connected with marriage. I felt no need to live with someone else.

But a person should have a place where he can warm himself, where he can relax and let down his guard. When Furman died, I became more and more restless. The thought of marriage lay on the surface. Irina was suitable for me: she was good, patient, tender; she understood me and supposedly had proven that she knew how to wait. I decided that it was best to go with the flow and we married.

Marriage in no way should have reflected on the external character of my life—I made this clear from the start. When our son was born a year later, his birth filled my soul with enormous warmth, but again it was not reflected in external circumstances. As before, I was constantly wrapped up in traveling, playing, and business affairs. But I began to get the feeling that something was happening to our family. I began to hear that I was traveling too often, and when I was home, I didn't lift a finger to help. What's true is true: I'm not very handy around the house. On the other hand, I took upon myself all concerns connected with the material side of our life, and that carries a lot of weight in the Soviet Union. But Irina had already stopped listening to the voice of reason. She wanted me to stay home like other "normal husbands."

As in the past, I continued to take her to tournaments, and then I decided to give her a good shock and I took her with me to Merano, Italy, followed by Argentina. Along the way I showed her Paris, and on the way home we stopped for a week in Italy where my friends arranged a wonderful visit for us to all the most beautiful places.

But this only postponed the crisis. Upon returning home, I understood that it was now impossible to pretend as if nothing were happening, so we spoke our minds. We had a son, and for this alone I was prepared to make great concessions. I remembered what my father was to me at this age—and still is to this day! But Irina was adamant. Somehow I managed to persuade Irina that we would restore a normal family life. Unfortunately, she took my initiative as a sign of weakness and expected concessions only from me. She fancied that now my attention to her should practically assume the forms of courting. Maybe I had become too businesslike over the years, but such a strenuous effort was beyond my power. In 1983 Irina and I split up for good.

The break-up of our family was a terrible blow. The loss of my son is a constant pain. Circumstances rarely permit me to see him, and so I remember him most of all when he was little. I remember how he learned to distinguish the chess pieces, how later he began to play chess, and then lost interest in it. He was attracted to screws, nuts, and bolts, any mechanical item. So he didn't turn out a chess player. It's not the first time. I know of many chess families—for example, the Petrosian, Geller, and Taimanov families—where the fathers tried to pass down their experience and skills, but this always ended in failure. Maybe love for chess skips a generation. We'll have to wait and see.

In that same year of 1983 I met my current wife,

Natasha Bulanov. I couldn't help but notice her. If at first she attracted me with her Russian beauty, then later it was with her good and kind heart. I quickly attached myself to her and we met every time I returned to Moscow from tournaments abroad. I could have proposed long ago, but having been hurt once, I was skittish. I saw that she understood my fear, and although it wasn't easy for her at times, I went slowly.

Four years later, I married her, and I'm very glad I did. In the years that we have been living together my attitude toward the home has changed. I felt I had a home, and I always returned to it with joy and relief. When at some distant tournament I remember Natalya's eyes and the look with which she greets me, my fatigue immediately disappears.

Natasha travels with me to the most important competitions: I'm convinced of her ability to soothe and relax me. And what is very rare for a pretty woman is that during contests she knows how to stay in the background and not make her presence felt. She appears only when the need arises. She graduated from the Institute of Historical Archives and works in the Lenin Library in the manuscripts division. She has very interesting work: since the Russian intelligentsia in the nineteenth century wrote and spoke French better than Russian, in addition to her decent English, she is studying French and is beginning to read the French classics.

I love her and sympathize with her very much. I understand how difficult it must be for an intelligent and creative woman to be with a businesslike person like me. Whenever I think of her, I see her with a book—sometimes reading, sometimes glancing up at me with her loving look.

I recognize that my wife has her own world. I could probably understand it, but for this I would have to leave mine, which unfortunately I will never do. Because her life, a life among harmony and beauty, is not for me.

CHAPTER SEVEN

ONLY ONE SUBJECT REMAINS TO REPORT ON: the history of my struggle against Kasparov.

This task places me in a difficult position. It's so recent a history, and anyone who has followed it remembers it. Therefore I'm not sure that I can say anything new. Much has already been written about our rivalry—the most prolific of its writers is Kasparov himself.

Of course, thanks to the press, not only the texts of our games, but their atmosphere and our behavior—good and not so good—will go down in history. Still, time strips away the trivial, leaving only the texts. Alekhine's match with Capablanca was exaggerated and colorfully depicted, but sixty years have passed, and now only chess historians remember the peripherals of that grandiose drama, and for 99 percent of the fans even their names are only symbols. It wouldn't be a bad thing to remember this, in order to put today's events in perspective.

With Kasparov and me, it wasn't so much the chess that entertained the public as it was what was going on around us. This always seemed vulgar to me. I can understand Kasparov and his need to return again and again to the episodes of our struggle. In essence, this was the only thing he had—only the fight with me, only the ceaseless squabbles, only the bewilderment that I won't surrender to him in any way, that I won't withdraw into the wings.

Because of my sporting connivance, because of my Slavic laziness, Kasparov became world champion, although theoretically he should not have. I admit that I have responded to our combat without disciplined responsibility. In order for him to beat me, he wrung himself dry and everyone else who could bring him the slightest advantage. He did it all with great economy and caution. And I just couldn't gather myself together to fight him effectively. Not in the first match when, leading five to nothing, I let him slip out from under my pressure; not in the fourth, in Seville, when all I had to do to have the title returned to me was to play out just one game to a draw. But instead I played the game carelessly; Kasparov played it halfheartedly, too, giving me real chances on several occasions to salvage a draw, but I didn't take advantage of any of them. As Korchnoi says, there are days when it is better not to sit down at the board at all.

For six years now I've tried to kindle anger in myself toward Kasparov and fuse my anger into a sword with which I can truly smite him at least once, but I can't. He's just not interesting to me, and that's all there is to it. Each time before I sit down with him at the board, all I have to do is remember that he'll begin to perform his theatrical pieces, he'll affect a deep meditation, torments, and hesitation, even though he knows every move in advance and is only performing during a game. You can be sure this spectacle is not for me—Kasparov understands that I know his worth—but for the public, and yet I can't deal with the annoying fact that I have to be part of it.

If only I had had my duel with Fischer, my fighting level would be of a higher order. Once I had attained and mastered such a level—a level which for Kasparov is completely unattainable—I would have easily recalled it whenever necessary. But I know for certain that on my own I will never elevate myself to it. At times I'm angry that Kasparov received his stimulus for perfection and for his supergame from me and my game, but I never had such a chance and now I never will.

My attitude toward chess literature used to be different. It was interesting for me to relate how a subject develops. Later I became more occupied with the psychology of battle. Obviously, this was dictated by life itself. Previously I played against the pieces, and then I began to consider the opponent's personality. But time passed, and I started to think less about the person sitting across the board from me and more about myself. Suddenly I understood that I knew much less about myself than I suspected, even less than I knew about my opponents. I realized that until I knew myself, I was destined to make the same mistakes again and again.

Kasparov has played a large role in my life. Since all the texts of our numerous chess games are easily obtainable, I won't go into them.

Kasparov was born in 1963. He likes to say he is a child of changes, the child of a new age, an age that gave birth to him, that made possible what he has become.

That is why he serves the business of change both in his country and in chess throughout the whole world.

Our conscientious soldier of *perestroika* was born only one year before Brezhnev came to power, a year before the inauguration of a truly stagnant period in our country. Consequently, in school, in films and books, on the radio and television, day after day he was absorbing crude hypocritical propaganda. As soon as he began to understand what was going on around him, the Soviet dual morality, cultivated everywhere—say one thing and think another—entered his soul effortlessly. This was the only way to get anywhere in life at that time. I wonder what might have become of him if, after coming of age and getting his passport, he had decided to live by his conscience instead. Even at twenty years of age he didn't make any pretenses to this, because *perestroika* wasn't even at the door yet, because we hadn't even dreamed of it.

His favorite theme is the inattention shown him by the authorities in childhood and adolescence, and the persecution and oppression suffered in adulthood. The child broke through to himself, he said, the child reached manhood in an uninterrupted and arduous struggle for existence. How was it in reality?

I know of no other grand master in our country, or the world, who has received such all-encompassing, massive support from the authorities. He had barely begun to stand out among his contemporaries when he was assigned a personal trainer, Aleksandr Shakarov, whose salary was paid by the Azerbaijan Sports Committee. At the age of thirteen he received a stipend as a young talented chess player, and by the following year the government had assigned another coach to him, Aleksandr Nikitin. For Shakarov and Nikitin Kasparov was their only job, day and night. The state paid for everything. Finally, Kasparov's mother was freed from her job as an engineer and put on the payroll as a chess specialist. To be sure, it wasn't a badly conceived idea, for the good of the cause and to create the most favorable regime for the youth, to have the mother devote herself entirely to her son. But I doubt seriously whether Klara Shagenovna had any notion of the difference between, say, the Nimzo-Indian Defense and the Queen's Indian Defense. In the West such a thing wouldn't have even occurred to anyone. If a young talent is insufficiently provided for, then those responsible for him try to raise his stipend, but what do parents have to do with it? With us and our Soviet system, these wonders are all in the normal course of things.

By 1976, when Gary was only thirteen, he already had complete say on where and when his training sessions would take place. The bill was unconditionally footed by the Azerbaijan Sports Committee or directly by the Azerbaijan Council of Ministers.

So where, then, did the authorities hinder him as he has said?

As soon as possible he was sent to a World Junior Championship, which he won. After this he began traveling regularly to international tournaments, something very few chess players in their junior years were able or allowed to do. In those years it was extremely difficult for a junior to go to a tournament outside the country, but for Kasparov this question was moot. So it should come as no surprise that by 1980 he was already a grandmaster. After this, in spite of his youth, he was freely admitted to the country's first team.

Perhaps not everyone knows that Kasparov was not always Kasparov. He used to be Weinstein, his father's surname. This name wasn't an obstacle for him; as Weinstein he received stipends, coaches, and training sessions. I don't know what would have happened if his father hadn't passed away. Either Kasparov himself or someone in his circle hit upon the idea that in the Soviet Union it's more convenient to be Kasparov (his mother's maiden name) than Weinstein. From a commercial point of view, I can understand this. But what about pride, and the memory of his father? Maybe I'm being petty, but for me it is precisely from such actions that a man defines himself.

As far as Kasparov's path to the Communist Party—

If he was such a nihilist, such a champion of truth, then he would have remained that way at least within his own conscience. In 1981—the apotheosis of stagnation in the country, with the party its embodiment— everything vital was being driven from the land, people were silenced with drugs in psychiatric hospitals, and others were rotting in prisons and concentration camps. It's understandable that few people had the courage to protest. If Gary was so honest, then at least he could have stepped aside and privately rebelled. But Gary is not like that. He knew he had to build his career, but to be in the USSR without a party membership card means no career. There was no line between chess and politics. Then they were one and the same. He had barely turned eighteen (the qualifying age) when he was already in the party, and without the obligatory candidate's length of service. In those years it was no easy thing to enter the party without passing a strict selection and elimination process. If it came so easily for him, then it has to mean that it was seriously prepared for and planned out in advance.

Despite human complexity, every person undoubtedly has one trait to which, like spokes of a wheel, all the others are connected. And if this hub can be named and understood, then a person seems to become more accessible and predictable. For example, a miser can be brave, sentimental, and philosophical. But if he is most of all a miser, you already know that his bravery is calculating, his sentimentality serves for self-justification, and his philosophy is just to convince himself of the vanity of any values, which are just substitutes for money anyway.

It was never easy for me with Kasparov.

I wanted to say "difficult," but that's not the case. Difficult is when a common denominator is sought, when there is dialogue and some sort of connection. But Kasparov and I have nothing in common. We were formed in different eras, I in the year of social renaissance and the emancipation of the populace's soul, and he in a time of stagnation. I came from the simple people and for a long time I remained one of them. He was singled out in childhood; elitism became an essential part of his world. For me chess was the end, for him it has merely been the means.

Even before our matches, I looked carefully at Kasparov and gave a great deal of thought to why he gives me so much trouble. I understood the reason: He's unprincipled. The environment, the times, and his upbringing made him a person who changes constantly according to given circumstances. At any moment he is exactly the type of person the situation requires. He can't be counted on, for at any moment he may slip away and change his point of view or guise. His main concern is advantage.

At the olympiad in Lucerne, when our whole team practically forced Kasparov to play Black against Ribli, how he fought against playing this game! What hysterics he raised! He called Moscow for advice, almost in tears. Then he became infuriated and began to threaten us, saying that when we returned to Moscow he'd introduce us to people who would wipe the floor with our faces, and no one could save us. But the interests of the team and the educational principle involved were higher, and we made Kasparov play this game. After the opening he found himself in the worst position. This brought him to his senses and he defended himself very adroitly. Ribli had only to offer a draw for Kasparov to agree to it immediately. He was happy that he'd gotten out of it. He was actually in a position to win the game, but he didn't see it. He was so afraid of Ribli that he sought only salvation.

About two years ago FIDE experienced its latest crisis, provided by Kasparov, and it was then that I recalled an old, but common, episode in chess. It happened in Malta during a chess olympiad. The affairs of our team weren't going too well. We were in pursuit of the Hungarians, but on that day we were to play the Bulgarian team. At one of the previous olympiads relations with the Bulgarian chess players had been exacerbated, not through any fault of our own. Tringov, in adjourning his game with Korchnoi, absentmindedly placed his sealed move in his pocket instead of an envelope, and the result was scandal. So we expected a bitter fight with them.

Kasparov, playing against Krum Georgiev, chose a sharp tactical variation in the Sicilian Defense, even though we had advised him against this—in a quiet tactical battle Kasparov stood a better chance. Georgiev found a "hole" in his strategy and outplayed him. He was only two or three obligatory moves away from a win, but, lost in thought, he grabbed for the wrong piece. He immediately corrected himself and made the correct move, but Kasparov rightfully insisted that the piece which had been touched should be moved. Again, a scandal ensued.

Although there was not a single eyewitness, the Bulgarian team stood up for their compatriot. You would have thought their eyes had never left the board. For many years now I've observed such incidents among chess players, but I never can get used to it. Naturally, a chivalrous spirit also exists in chess but its traditions are becoming weaker by the day. For the sake of the outcome, many are prepared nowadays to call Black White, and vice versa, without giving it a second thought.

This, however, is not the point. It just so happened that I was looking in that direction and saw almost everything. Moreover, Georgiev wasn't a very good actor. He slouched awkwardly but then, sensing the support of his teammates, he gradually straightened up. Since I was an interested eyewitness, an objective observer had to be found. But there was none. And then suddenly grand master Kirov produced Lincoln Lucena, president of the Central American Zone. Here, he said, is your neutral witness; he saw everything. Lucena, not batting an eye, confirmed it. Yes, I saw everything, Kasparov is wrong and is raising a fuss only because he is a sore loser. But

I knew that at the moment of the rule violation Lucena was far away and could not possibly have seen a thing.

What could chief arbiter Lothar Schmid do? He was forced to admit that Georgiev was correct, and Kasparov stopped his clock a few moves later.

After such an incident I don't have to explain how Lucena presents himself in a moral plan. Kasparov, who suffered from his "adherence to principle," should know and understand this well. I was certain that for Kasparov Lucena would simply cease to exist as a person. But six years passed, and Kasparov needed an ally in his battle against Campomanes. Here he counted upon Lucena and spared no efforts, campaigning for him with representatives of each federation. With all his eloquence he praised Lucena, emphasizing his honesty and principles. One thing is true: Tell me who your friend is, and I'll tell you who *you* are.

Another time, due to political games, the challenger matches between Kasparov and Korchnoi and Ribli and Smyslov almost fell through. This was a difficult time. It was 1983 and, as a result of our invasion of Afghanistan, relations with the United States were extremely strained. For the Kasparov-Korchnoi match, Holland, Spain, and the United States made bids. Korchnoi chose Holland and Kasparov chose Spain. What was Campomanes to do? He decided not to give anyone preference and proposed the match be held in Pasadena, California, where, incidentally, the prize money was highest. Korchnoi accepted this offer, as did Kasparov, albeit unofficially (his acceptance was conveyed through grand master Marovic, with whom Kasparov was then writing a book). Campomanes flew to Pasadena to prepare for the match. When everything had been settled and the agreements signed, he informed our Soviet Chess Federation. Out of political considerations (the question of whether to boycott the upcoming Olympics in Los Angeles had been decided "upstairs") our federation told Kasparov to refuse, which he did without hesitation. An exchange of telexes followed. Campomanes insisted that he had Kasparov's consent and that this decision was the most reasonable one. Our side replied that Kasparov hadn't known anything about the agreement and that there could be no further discussion of Pasadena as a site for the match. Campomanes then flew to Moscow, and, in a personal meeting with Kasparov, one-on-one and in the presence of witnesses, Kasparov, with his usual volatile nature, announced that he would give his official agreement only to Spain, that he had never conducted any unofficial negotiations, and that he supported in full the political position of our federation.

I was an unwilling participant in these negotiations. I was asked to threaten Campomanes. If he didn't come over to our side, I was also supposed to refuse to play the match for the World Championship. The pressure on me was terrible. Naturally, I wouldn't have any part of this dirty game, but, making use of my good relations with Campomanes, I did everything I could to smooth over the conflict somehow and salvage the matches.

The talks lasted all night. An agreement was reached concerning the Ribli-Smyslov match, and at seven the next morning Campomanes flew out of Moscow. By nine o'clock a telex was sent after him stating that this agreement was *also* invalid. The initiator of this action was Kasparov. At the last moment he said that if the second match took place, then failure to appear at the match with Korchnoi would mean a loss. He demanded that Gramov, chairman of the Soviet Sports Committee, annul the agreement of Smyslov's match. All this—the repudiation of his word and, let's call things by their true names, his betrayal of his older colleague—took place in the course of just one night. No matter how many telegrams Gramov sent afterward to the Communist Party Central Committee, the Council of Ministers, and the Kremlin, there was no response. Kasparov wasn't on his own, and Gramov met him halfway not because he was Kasparov, but because behind this young man loomed a dark figure in those years, the omnipotent Geidar Aliev.

Further sudden reversals in fortune during this incident are extraordinarily complex. It ended in disgrace for our federation and sports committee. In order to save the matches in which Kasparov and Smyslov would be credited with defeats for not playing, the FIDE governing body was presented with official written apologies and a fine of 160,000 rubles. The money was paid by direct order of Aliev. I would like to know what other government would so easily pay such sums for its lack of principles and the stupidity of its bureaucrats. After this, Kasparov, with a straight face, claimed that the state and its administrative system were always against him and did everything in their power to stop him. Even if there had been such a plan, in which administrative chicanery would not let him near a match with me, this match would never have taken place. One stroke of the pen would have been sufficient to break it. Then, Kasparov was nothing more than a capable young chess player with an unstable psyche, but sufficiently obedient so as not to fall out of step with the grandiose state system in which he had resourcefully found a place.

There are many witnesses to confirm how much I did

for these matches to take place, not only for the sake of Smyslov, whom I like and respect, or because this candidates' cycle was going to be his last. I simply wanted everything to be on the up and up. Of course, I "risked" taking Kasparov's wrath upon myself. I don't accidentally place "risked" in quotations—Kasparov then was still not a serious challenger to me. I saw all his weaknesses and didn't doubt that I'd deal with him without any special effort. This match was in my interest, for the earlier we met, the more resounding the rout would be. I would have given this impressionable young person an inferiority complex, and a lot of time would have passed before he would have been able to rid himself of this complex.

While the fate of his match with Korchnoi was problematic, Kasparov consulted me, sought my support, and considered it natural to visit me at home. I even had to make an inconvenient trip to the Philippines. We all figured that in the interests of the matter it would be a sin not to exploit my good relations with Campomanes. The plan worked. But hardly had the difficulties been set aside when another Kasparov took over, replacing the first. The first bell sounded in London, where his match was played with Korchnoi. The organizers invited me as an honored guest, and we agreed that I would give a speech in the clubs of parliamentarians and businessmen. Scarcely had I arrived in London when an employee of the Soviet embassy officially reported to me that my stay there was undesirable and it was suggested that I leave the city immediately.

I know that all this must seem like nonsense, and my departure slavish obedience. That's all true. Today nobody would dare to demand such things, but if it did happen, I wouldn't think twice about doing it. Back then disobedience was cause for the most serious concern and fear. I wouldn't have been allowed to travel abroad. The fact that I was the world champion wouldn't have made it any easier for me.

I asked for an explanation of my expulsion. It turned out that Kasparov told Moscow that if I were to appear at the match, Korchnoi would be enraged and transfer his negative attitude from me to him. "Fine," I said. "I won't attend the match. But I have some business in London and I'm obliged to stay on." "No. It is suggested that you leave London," said the embassy employee sternly, "and the sooner, the better."

I'm on friendly terms with our ambassador to Great Britain. This time I decided not to put him in an awkward position, but on the next trip, in view of the fact that things had changed, I asked him what had happened then. It was revealed that Kasparov, having found out about my arrival, got in touch with the aide to the all-powerful Aliev, after which an "opinion" was sent down to the chairman of the sports committee, Gramov, who in turn gave the order: Get Karpov out of there.

The next strange episode wasn't long in coming. It happened after Kasparov won a Candidates Finals Match, leading to a match between us. I was preparing for a match in Bugojno, which is a very prestigious and serious tournament; I took first place there in 1978 and 1980. Kasparov won it in 1982, when I did not participate, there being no rule that specified the tournament's past winner must be invited. Now I learned that Kasparov insisted on participating in none other than this tournament. For his successful preparation in the upcoming match against me, he said that he needed to play in strong company, and nothing was better than this. I was asked about it, and I answered that if he really needed it that much, then, for God's sake, let him play there. But since I don't consider it possible to play a tournament alongside a future opponent, I would have to find something else for myself.

Before I announced this, the organizers of the tournament were euphoric. They were going to get both the world champion *and* the challenger. When I refused, they called me again.

"Please return to the tournament."

"But you know my reasons," I answered. "Because of the upcoming match I don't want to play in the same tournament with the challenger."   `

"But he's not playing," they told me. "When you refused, he also dropped out." I went on to play at tournaments in London and Olso instead of Bugojno.

Still, judge for yourselves why Kasparov needed this whole incident. Did he have to prove to himself that he could single-handedly oust me from any tournament?

I think that the entire moral experience of mankind is contained for Kasparov in a well-known formula: Might makes right. If you look closely at his actions over the years, it's easy to see that he took it into his head to rebuild the chess world according to his own standards of truth, goodness, and beauty. He began almost immediately after he beat me in the Moscow match and was proclaimed the world champion.

The fact is that before any match the participants always sign an agreement obliging themselves to fulfill the corresponding regulations of FIDE. Our agreement contained a paragraph about a return match, in the event I lost. And that's what happened—I lost. Automatically the condition for a return match was put into effect. We had to agree on its conditions, times, and dates. Suddenly Kasparov announced that he was not going to play it.

The resolution of this issue took place at a session of the Presidium of the USSR Chess Federation. Kasparov was asked, "What's the problem? You signed the agreement, including the part about a return match. How can you refuse to cooperate? Your signature is here." Kasparov answered, "I signed it as the challenger. Now I'm the champion, and I consider all signatures made up to this point to be invalid."

Kasparov's portrait would be incomplete if I didn't include his characteristic vindictiveness. One victim of this vindictiveness was the grandmaster Eduard Gufeld, a favorite among chess players around the world for his joviality and sharp-wittedness. Not long before the episode I'm about to relate, he had published a large laudatory book on Kasparov.

It happened right after the match in Seville. I had played the last game unsuccessfully, Kasparov evened the score, and, according to FIDE rules, since the match didn't produce a clear winner, the title of world champion was retained by him.

This last game was far from being a masterpiece of chess art. It was poor in ideas and rich in mistakes. But Kasparov kept pressuring me and I got into time trouble. Kasparov decided to take advantage of this, successfully sacrificing a pawn, but then he became excited and played imprecisely. I was presented with a beautiful chance to seize the initiative. Just one accurate move, which I could see, but for some reason I considered impossible. If I had done it, White (Kasparov) would have had to struggle tortuously for a draw. And then I would have been world champion again. But I didn't have time; I miscalculated, chose an unsure plan, and lost.

Saved at the very last moment and excited by the fact that he was still world champion, Kasparov opened his heart to Gufeld in an interview immediately following the game. At a certain moment, he said, he understood that the game was moving toward a draw, and he embarked on a combination which was a bluff. Gufeld reported it all in the newspaper *Sovetskii Sport*.

Shortly thereafter, after he had returned home and calmed down, Kasparov found the confidence to call the Seville draw nothing other than his victory; he had decided that the admission of a bluff was damaging to his chess dignity. The fact that he himself had called it a bluff meant nothing to him. Gufeld had written this, so Gufeld had devalued his victory in the decisive game: Gufeld had to be punished.

Kasparov didn't have to look for an opportunity. Gufeld was getting ready to go to England, where he was invited to the annual Hastings Tournament. He already had both his visa and ticket. But Kasparov called the sports committee and demanded that Gufeld, for humiliating his dignity, not be allowed out of the country. I learned of the call from the committee's deputy chairman, V. Gavrilin. A day before he was scheduled to leave, Gufeld appeared at the sports committee, where he was told that his visa had been annulled. This reprehensible stunt wouldn't have come off with anybody else, but Kasparov got away with it. Gufeld related this entire story to me.

From Kasparov's side this action was particularly foul, because he *knew* that Gufeld's trip to England also involved family matters. His son had married an Englishwoman and was living there. Gufeld filed a protest with the newspaper and with the Association of Grandmasters, of which Kasparov was the president. Attempting to avoid a discussion of this conflict, Kasparov wiggled like a garden snake, but a letter existed and he had to answer it. Naturally, if you're not caught, you're not a thief. So he denied everything.

I already said it once, and I'll say it again: I don't believe in deviltry. I believe that things depend on how you feel—things that are revealed at the most inopportune moment, that can't be controlled. I believe in fatigue, which sneaks up on you quietly, and suddenly you don't have the power to change anything.

Perhaps there is something to the supersensitive possibilities of our psyches. Otherwise, I can't explain the many coincidences which occurred in my matches with Kasparov, coincidences which I found out about only two years ago. I have to admit that had it not been for the parapsychologist Dadashev, Kasparov might not be world champion.

Dadashev appeared at our first match when I was leading four to nothing. In the first match Kasparov didn't have the steadfastness and depth he displayed in the Seville match. Without a doubt, he is a very talented and a very strong chess player, but there were huge gaps in his chess education, which I managed to uncover in the beginning of the match. People say that my goal—to win six to nothing—was my downfall. Perhaps. But if, after victory in the twenty-seventh game, when the score stood at five to nothing, I had won in the thirty-first, then of course everyone would have proclaimed this a brilliant match.

In chess, as in life, most evaluation is conducted in retrospect, and it is directly tied to a result. Success, and you're a hero, and everything you did was beautiful. Lack of success, and history will gladly find flaws, despite your best effort.

I didn't manage to get to my goal, but even now I'm convinced that I played correctly. I repeat: If I had won the thirty-first game, I would have been right all around; in the forty-first I again could have won forcedly in a few moves, and again all the reproaches would have been lifted. But at certain moments it's as if I were replaced by someone else. Fantastic unluckiness, and inexplicably sudden blindness, and my hopes turned to dust.

Short draws didn't bother me. They mainly arose when I was playing Black. As White I constantly caused problems for Kasparov. Gradually the tension diminished due to fatigue. If at this time I had gone over to a sharp game, I could have lost a game, maybe two, but without a doubt I would have won a sixth, and with it the match. I understood this, too, but I can't explain why I rejected any thoughts of such playing in the second half of the match. The easiest solution is to blame all this stubborn passive thinking on Dadashev.

Most of the discussion in this book concerning parapsychological activity around the chessboard has focused on Baguio. I don't know what the skilled craftsmen helping Kasparov were capable of, but Professor Zukhar, who had accompanied me, had absolutely no relation at all to parapsychology. He is an eminent psychologist who has studied sleep and dreams, as well as questions of learning foreign languages in one's sleep. His reputation was clean, and for all the decades of his work he was never cited in any quasiscientific activity.

Dadashev is a different matter. He is a parapsychologist and a well-known one at that, famous the world over for his appearance at the 1973 Prague Congress of Parapsychologists, where his demonstrations astounded his American colleagues. In those years he was recognized as being first among the world's parapsychologists. Then it turned out that he had hooked up with Kasparov at a time when I was leading four to nothing in the first match. Dadashev took an active part in our three matches, but I found out about it only from Dadashev himself when he came to see me not long before the match in Seville and confessed to his interference in our duel.

"I didn't do anything bad to you," he assured me. "I only helped Kasparov. You understand that these are two completely different things. Kasparov seemed to me so pure, inexperienced, and naïve. He was so confused; he needed support. But now I see that this was only a mask, because he makes use of his situation not for good, as I had hoped. No, he breeds evil. But I didn't harm you, believe me. Our professional code does not allow it."

Perhaps, but in one of our conversations, he told me himself how he discovered his talent in childhood. He was in school and was having problems with a teacher. Then one day, when an inspection commission visited the class, the boy sensed that now was the time he could get even for all the trouble she had caused him. He didn't know exactly how but he fixed his gaze on her and began suggesting: Make a mistake! Make a mistake! And she did. That boy didn't know any parapsychologists' code of honor.

Dadashev brought me his manuscript, called *Revelation*. I was dumbstruck as I read it. I couldn't imagine that such powers truly exist, but here were things that can't be thought up, known only to a select few who were privy to the heart of the match. Then there were the photographs of Kasparov with fervent inscriptions like "For your invaluable help in the match," "For your support and help in the twenty-second game of the return match in Leningrad," as well as tickets which Kasparov sent him, not the usual admission tickets, but complimentary, with the stamp of the administration, doled out to each of the teams in advance in a fixed quantity. From these tickets I could now accurately picture where he sat, and, inasmuch as over the years I had developed the habit of looking over the hall carefully, especially the seats of the opposing team, I remembered him. He was present at these games with his piercing gaze. I distinctly recalled his obtrusive presence at the last game of the second match, the game after which I lost the title of world champion. So, Professor, you say that you only helped Kasparov, but didn't try to bother me?

Dadashev published an article in *Der Spiegel* in 1987 explaining how he had helped me against Kasparov in Seville. As opposed to our 1984–85 match, Dadashev was not present in the spectators' hall in Seville, nor was he even in the country when we played, and he did not exert any influence on either Kasparov or me.

Much was written about Dadashev. Not long before the Seville match a book appeared in Baku, capital of the republic of Azerbaijan, written in Azerbaijani and entitled *The Dadashev Phenomenon*. Gary Kasparov wrote the book's foreword. It was supposed to have been published in a Russian translation, but Kasparov learned about *Revelation* and publication was halted.

Revelation also had an unhappy printing history. It could have been a best-seller. Newspaper and magazine editors eagerly snatched at the manuscript, read it excitedly, and promised to publish it, but it never went any further than that. Only now has *Revelation* broken through, on the pages of the newspaper *Vechernyaya Kazan'*. Somewhere, apparently, something in Kasparov's system didn't work and a slip-up occurred. Usually his team didn't allow such mistakes.

I hope that by now it's at least somewhat clear why I'm in no hurry to describe our rivalry. I'm working on the chess commentaries to these games, many of which have already been published. But everything that's separate from chess is still too unclear. Most likely, someone else will always want to dig around in it, but so far I'm not interested. The time hasn't come. The dust hasn't settled.

Maybe this is intuition talking to me: Don't hurry, it's saying, the story will end on a happy note, and *then* you can write. That would be good. Not just for me, but for everyone, this battle evokes a feeling of something that is held back. It would be fine if this feeling were confirmed by life. I know that it depends only upon me.

With every year, the ascent to the familiar peak arouses in me less and less ardor. Everything there is already familiar. But our contemporary life will bring so much that's new that it will be impossible to feel bored, all the more so now that I'm a People's Deputy, something I'm very serious about. I like to be among people and I like to help them. Sometimes when I'm with them and wrapped up in their affairs, I even forget about chess, but people always remind me. They are interested in how my preparations are going for the next storm. I'm always struck by this interest of theirs toward me, a total stranger to them, and their interest in a game about which they know so little. I've thought about this more than once and this is what I've decided: It's not a question of me, or even of chess. It's because in my struggle I'm an example to them in something. They are pulling for me, as if they've guessed that if it works out for me, then it will work out for them, too. Now, really, how can I let them down?

CHAPTER EIGHT

IT'S NOT A PLEASANT TASK to have to analyze the reasons for a defeat that might not have been, that should not have been.

If someone had asked me on the eve of the last match to compare the conditions of the world champion's preparations with those of the challenger, I probably would have enumerated all the main points that I am going to address now. I have played the role of champion and the role of challenger. I know all the tricks, all the pluses and minuses. Why haven't I written about this until now? The answer is that this book was conceived and created during the last championship cycle and, although I expected difficulties in my match with Kasparov, I was full of hope; I believed in my ultimate success. Although defeat was, of course, possible, I drove the thought from my mind. Yet it did happen. Now I realize that I can no longer avoid the subject.

"Champion" and "challenger" are nothing more than titles, coordinates by which to determine the position of any athlete on a concrete hierarchical ladder: university champion, city or national champion, world champion. Yet the rules of conduct between champion and challenger in chess are unlike those in other sports. In boxing, for instance, no one would think to discuss (let alone defend) the privileges of the champion over the challenger. There is the ring, the boxers are the same weight, they wear identical gloves, and the judges evaluate them as equals for the duration of the bout. Whoever is stronger during that time is awarded the victory. God forbid it should become known that one of the boxers had some kind of advantage over the other, whether a weight advantage, use of steroids, or the sympathy of the judges.

The match for the world chess championship is a different matter altogether. Here, inequality is at the foundation of the whole system. It is a historical fact. No one seems concerned about this; everyone assumes that it cannot be any other way. Unequal conditions for champion and challenger in chess have always existed. Inequality was even a part of Botvinnik's system. Naturally, over time the degree of inequality has changed, but on the whole it has continued to live on and be observed. The difference is that in the past this inequality wasn't as keenly felt as it is now.

The main problem is that the world champion does not have to win in order to retain his title. All he has to do is play the match out to a draw, and he keeps everything. Please understand me correctly: I'm not lobbying for any privileges for the challenger; rather, that there should be no privileges for anyone. If you do not win, then at this date and place you were weaker. With our current rules, however, while a player may not have it in him to prove his superiority, he may still be considered the champion. This is a typical example of the triumph of rules over common sense. Yet this can be resolved simply by agreeing to play additional games if the first match ends in a draw. These games might even be played according to the rules of speed chess.

Although this problem has existed for a long time, I have not raised the issue until now because I did not see any urgency to it. For as long as I was champion the system was advantageous to me, of course. Others did not mention it and I held my tongue. (It was a compromise with conscience, but not such a big one as to suffer unduly from it.) When I became the challenger I reconciled myself to the reduction in rights. I even felt that in some way I had to pay for the advantages I had enjoyed as champion. But on the eve of the last match this problem grew to such dimensions that I was no longer able to keep silent about it.

My previous match with Kasparov, in Seville, had ended in a draw. Kasparov, according to the existing rules, retained his title of champion even though he did not beat me. Fine. Still, it was an appropriate moment to ask the question: Who will be named world chess champion if the upcoming match also ends in a draw? Again, according to the rules, Kasparov should keep his title. Yet he hadn't even won the preceding match! He could, despite not having won a single match since 1986, remain world champion for as long as he liked by playing to draws in 1987, 1990, 1993, 1996, and so on.

It was clear that it made no difference who Kasparov's opponent would be. But it fell upon me to challenge him, and this only underscored the unjustness of the situation.

Why have I been silent until now? Perhaps because

of my conservatism; or my certainty that I can beat Kasparov cleanly; or my sense that chess society is not ready to take such a radical step.

I was prepared to make this statement, but I might not have dared to do so this soon had I not been provoked by Kasparov. It happened in New York at the prematch press conference. Kasparov tried to make an impression on the journalists with his confidence and aplomb. He announced that this match would not produce just a victory—he was going to crush me. He was so certain of his obvious superiority and, consequently, his win.

I had heard this so many times before that one would think that I would have been used to it by now. On this occasion, however, I couldn't take it any longer. Kasparov had been a bit too garrulous. It would have been a sin to let it pass without proving to everyone what in fact was hiding behind those words.

Overcoming my fear, I decided to make an announcement: If Kasparov is indeed so certain of his huge superiority, then I find it hard to understand why he hangs on to this dubious privilege that allows him to keep his world champion's title in the event of a draw. At every opportunity he proclaims himself a fighter for democracy, justice, and equal rights for all. But let him put his money where his mouth is and agree to a simple concession: refuse the undeserved handicap and, in this case at least, make our rights equal.

His response surpassed all my expectations. Unable to disentangle himself to express a clear thought, he resorted to his usual tactics: His temperamental, fiery character took over. He literally howled. Here's the true Karpov, you see? Again he's looking for privileges for himself, again he's dodging in order to gain an advantage for himself. . . . In short, he was categorically and principally against any revision of the rules.

There is another tradition that exists only in chess. While the challengers duke it out among themselves for the right to play the champion, he sits atop the heap, waiting for the most successful one to emerge from the pack. Champions in other sports are honored, but as soon as the next championship season begins they start on an equal footing with the others, raising themselves up step by step to the next round.

Incidentally, the national chess champions of all countries participate in championships on equal conditions with the challengers. Only the world champion is exempt from this. Why? Again, such is the tradition, passed down from the first world champions who, from a position of strength, dictated their conditions to the challengers. Since then, however, the world and its mores have changed tremendously, the exchange of information has intensified a thousandfold, but, still, the tradition lives on steadfastly.

The privilege of the champion manifests itself in other ways, too. The challenger is forced to pass through the meat grinder of team competitions; the champion prepares for a match in whatever way pleases him. If he desires to prepare in private, then it is his prerogative. If he wants to control the level of preparation in tournaments, he can choose from among a huge field representing all levels of strength. He can bolster his confidence in weak tournaments or temper himself in the strongest competitions. And this is the most important point: By not revealing his cards (because in these competitions he is not obligated to win), he can observe all the hands of his opponents, the direction of their experiments, their weaknesses and strengths.

This produces an enormous inequality in terms of information. The days when it was possible to win a serious game only by merit of sporting character or depth of chess understanding have vanished forever. Chess knowledge has become dominant, bypassing all the other factors that contribute to success. It is available to everyone, and it often compensates for many other shortcomings. It is the result of true democratism in professional chess. Yet it was not always like this. In Botvinnik's time it was possible to develop an original idea and then use it to play a good tournament or match, sometimes even several in a row, before the idea was made generally available. Now this is impossible. Any game, especially a game played by one of the grandmasters, is subjected to simultaneous massive analysis by a hundred pairs of eyes in all corners of the globe. If therein lies an original idea, then literally the next day everyone knows it, and immediately sets to studying it, searching for an antidote, or its development, or something similar in other positions where this idea can be injected.

The world champion does not have this problem. He is not obliged to lay out his cards until the time to defend his title arrives. He can even allow himself a loss, just to keep from revealing himself.

But the challenger often has to lay out all of his baggage. In order to get to the match, he has to overcome opponents who are often not weaker than he is. These opponents are not stiffs you can outclass with technique and character. New methods are needed. You have to employ as many new methods as are needed, because if you are stingy now you may not make it to the championship. Occasionally you throw down your trump cards only to find that you are holding nothing special. This happened to me in the match against Artur Yusupov. I was struggling with unresolved problems. Meanwhile, Yusupov was the strongest he has ever been. I had to claw and scratch my way to the very end. I needed to use everything I had; nothing was hidden away in reserve.

On the other hand, in the match against Timman, I had practically no trouble at all. Some original ideas I had developed and used successfully allowed me to play a normal game. Is this good? Of course. But a bullet, once spent, cannot be used again. How I lacked for these bullets half a year later in the match against Kasparov. I had to play three matches to get to Kasparov. Three dozen games. I was forced to bare myself almost completely.

Kasparov, of course, had entirely different worries: While I prepared for Johann Hjarterson and fought against him, Kasparov was getting ready for Karpov. While I prepared for Yusupov and fought against him, Kasparov readied himself for Karpov. While I prepared for Timman and fought against him, Kasparov braced himself for Karpov. His entire entourage was focused on me. They studied me, sought breaches in my favorite formations, and looked for antidotes to my plans of attack—my plans and mine only. Of course, they followed the progress of the other challengers as well, since each one was a possible source for new ideas, too. But I am convinced that Kasparov did not see any of them as a possible opponent.

When I finally emerged to take on Kasparov, I had six months in which to get ready for the match. Naturally,

I had thought about it, hoping it would take place. As I said before, I believed that it would. But there was no work done specifically for the match, or for Kasparov. Survive, scratch, crawl to it, I told myself, and then we'll decide what and how to deal with it.

Half a year is not a small amount of time. But as soon as you begin to lay down a plan for the essential work, it breaks up into small pieces and suddenly it turns out that very little time is left. Therefore, you have to set priorities immediately. First, you have to rest. It's not so much a question of restoring your strength after the last match as it is a matter of distancing yourself from the game itself. Rest and removal from the game are needed just as much before the match itself. If freshness is lacking, and the desire to play or desire to fight is absent, then it's better not to sit down or to play at all.

Then one needs at least three months of preparation per se—for analysis of your opponent, and for the development of openings and new ideas. These have to be further broken down into working with White and Black, with the various types of openings, and themes within openings. In terms of preparation time, the world champion has a very big, if not decisive, advantage. Let me cite just one example. Playing Black, I put great stake in the Ruy Lopez: I like it, feel it, and understand it; in the matches with Hjarterson and Timman it served me well. Kasparov's group was on the receiving end of a rich lode of material and they made excellent use of it. During our match Kasparov won two games strictly as a result of home preparation in these variations. I had no time to fundamentally change my repertoire or work out something profoundly new. In a match between approximately equal opponents this disparity in preparation time is a huge handicap.

Where to play is always a problem. The site doesn't appear right away. First, sponsors and organizers have to be found, and only then is a decision made. New Zealand and Lyons had argued a long time for the right to hold the match. And then, suddenly, New York appeared, making offers to host just the first half of the match. Right off, I didn't like the idea. The London-Leningrad match, with the unpleasant feeling of incompletion after the London half, and the tortuous attempts to get back in tune again in Leningrad, was still fresh in my memory. Whoever assumes that it's no big deal for a match to be divided into two halves simply has no ideas how it disrupts the match's continuity.

However, the American offer had its indisputable advantages and to simply wave it off would have been unwise. I insisted upon a variant in which all the pluses were retained and all the obvious minuses kept to a minimum.

By a strange confluence of circumstances the most important negotiations concerning the match were set for precisely that moment when the vice presidents of the Grandmasters Association (GMA), Timman and I, were squaring off in the challengers' match. The final decision was made in our absence. There was nothing left for us to do but accept what was offered. The arrangement that was settled on, however, was not on the whole bad. At least it looked good on paper.

The plan, conceived no doubt with the best of intentions, had serious defects exactly at those points that were viewed as advantages. The two-week intermission ruined the natural flow of the match (and was hard on me physically). Moving the beginning of the match to October (also supposedly to my benefit by giving me a little more time to prepare) meant that we were to play through three different seasons—summer, autumn, and winter, with a temperature range of 86 to 5 degrees. Finally, my hopes for the objectivity of the organizers were justified. I relied upon them, but here Kasparov held the reins in his hands. He controlled every little detail, and, as events would prove, he did not miscalculate.

In May 1990 I met with the organizers of the upcoming match for the first time. One glance was enough to know that these were solid people and experienced organizers. No need to worry here. The psychological considerations, however, did not interest them at all. Chess, after all, is a battle of intellects and psychology plays a major role in it.

Robert Burkett was one of the main organizers. I trusted him immediately, but at our very first meeting he told me bluntly: We're not going to deny that we're fans of Kasparov; it's because of him we went into chess and because of him we took up the organization of this match. But don't let this bother you. We're going to observe neutrality and do everything possible for the opponents to reveal who is stronger under equal conditions. In Burkett's defense I have to admit that he kept his word, but, living full-time in Los Angeles as he did, there were, inevitably, details of the situation in New York that slipped out from under his control.

Strictly speaking, however, "control" was not under his jurisdiction; that was the prerogative of the patrons of the match, FIDE and GMA. They were obliged to make sure the rules were observed and to keep the conditions, set by the organizers, equal for the two sides.

A conflict broke out between FIDE and GMA over the issue of money. The underlying cause looked straight forward enough: Who will run the match? In practice, however, it meant: Who will stand closer to the till? FIDE won the battle, negotiating a 20 percent cut from the organizers to be set aside for the development of chess. But FIDE and GMA fastened onto the prize money. By agreement, both took 10 percent from each of the participants of the match. The size of the prize was immediately reduced by 20 percent for both Kasparov and me.

I am not disputing this. Chess must be supported, and if organizations take upon themselves certain headaches, they should be recompensed for it. Our patrons, however, limited themselves to choosing a site for the match and drawing up a contract, after which they washed their hands of the whole affair. No appeals or exhortations could move them from the position of detached observers. A glaring example of this is that Campomanes not only never once came to New York to check on the pre-match preparations but also—in violation of tradition—did not even attend the opening.

Problems arose in both New York and Lyons. To be sure, the problems would have been fewer had Kasparov and I defended our interests as a united front. But with him such a thing is possible only when interests are fully meshed.

Both of us attach great significance to publicity. I did not think that Kasparov would personally bother about questions of publicity during the course of the match, that he would not need to, since he had taken care of something more important ahead of time: the organizers of the match choose chess experts only from the retinue of Kasparov's worshipers and hangers-on. When I found out who was among them I began to protest, but FIDE and GMA had already put the matter behind them. I quickly understood that no one was going to bother changing the composition of the experts. That was the end of it. It was already done and other issues were at hand.

I warned the organizers that these guys would cause them a lot of problems. The match had not yet begun and so far they had only succeeded in preparing some official materials for the first press conference when a scandal erupted. The press release was biased, one-sided, and pro-Kasparov. He was presented as a kind of ideal, Americanized hero, a valiant fighter against corrupt power, the upholder of freedom and democracy. I, on the other hand, was characterized as a stalwart defender of communism and the totalitarian regime. Anticipating this, I had asked ahead of time to see the materials. After all, if they were going to distribute official information about me, they should at least have asked for my approval. No one did this. Kasparov's people controlled this process, but this time they had gone too far. The organizers found themselves in an awkward position and were forced to apologize.

Kasparov himself was not above getting involved in these affairs, as in the episode with grand master Yasser Seirawan, who offered his services to the match's organizers. He wanted to be a television commentator for the match. Kasparov knew about this and decided to make good use of it during an important vote at the General Assembly of the GMA, held in June 1990 at Murcia, Spain. Prior to the vote, Kasparov had carried out a great deal of preparatory work, acting where necessary with promises. When in private conversation Yasser let it be known that he did not agree with many of his directives, Kasparov abruptly switched the conversation over to the upcoming match and boasted that the organizers clearly stood on his side. The implication was that Yasser's work as a commentator literally depended upon one word from the world champion.

I have to give credit to the Western grand masters. They did not bow to Kasparov's politics, nor did they accept his program entirely. Seirawan was among those who voted against Kasparov. This infuriated him to such a degree that he was not ashamed to announce in the presence of eyewitnesses, "Yasser, tomorrow I'll fly to New York and meet with Burkett. I will report to him exactly what happened and how you voted. We will see how much work you do in New York!" He kept his word. (Seirawan made public this whole unbecoming story in his journal, *Inside Chess*.)

Every match is preceded by scandalous situations. Some arise spontaneously, others are planned, but in general a match never comes off without them. Kasparov and I also tried to uphold the ancient tradition and toss the journalists some choice morsels. For example, Kasparov made a demonstration with the Russian tricolor (nothing will ever convince me that he was serious about that), and I announced that I would prefer to avoid handshakes before and after games.

The match itself is so fresh in the minds of all who

took an interest in it that I do not see any reason to discuss in great detail the texts and commentaries of the games; a deeper understanding of it is still to come. One needs some distance to see the match in its entirety; only then will it be possible to appraise it objectively.

Nonetheless, several key moments stand out. The first game is always used for intelligence gathering, for checking yourself and your opponent, for checking stability, energy, depth, and mood. The game was fierce and compact. We both showed that we weren't opposed to winning right off the bat, but neither did we rush to do it: a win in the first game is a bad omen.

I lost the second game. Kasparov caught me with his home analysis. None of the spectators in the hall knew this. They only saw how Kasparov sweated, racked his brains, tormented himself, squeezed his temples. But during the game, information leaked from the press center that Kasparov's variation was being developed by his team right up to the moment of his sacrifice of a bishop—somewhere around the thirtieth to fortieth moves.

His plan turned out to be an excellent one. Give Kasparov's team praise for discovering and developing this variation and bolstering it with some profound analysis. As far as this game itself is concerned, it is all right to speak of an excellently conducted prematch preparation and of excellent home analysis. Just don't talk about the *playing*. Because the *playing* was only on one side— mine. Kasparov can only be lauded for *execution*.

It was a beautiful game, the defeat was convincing, and the novelty employed was simple and clever. This confirmed the commentators' most optimistic prognostications. They began predicting that within a few games I would break because Kasparov was brilliantly prepared; the novelties he possessed were too numerous to count, and no matter where I turned I would always be running up against them. In short, the day would finally come when it would be proven clearly to one and all that Kasparov had greatly surpassed me in chess, and that the difference in age between us of twelve years would be an immovable burden to me in the match.

Now it was incumbent upon Kasparov to justify the overtures and move quickly to secure his success. Judging by his mood before the fourth game, I understood that a melee was at hand, and I wasn't mistaken. The fourth game to a certain degree set the tone for the whole match.

I played a home-prepared variation. Kasparov responded very quickly, meaning that his team has also traversed this road at home. This put me on my guard. I slowed the pace and began to analyze the ostensibly familiar continuations when I suddenly discovered a hole in my analysis, a hole which Kasparov was undoubtedly aware of. It was not for nothing that he was driving me so assuredly toward it.

I quickly realized that I was standing with one foot over a pit. I pondered this position for about fifty minutes before finding a very sharp and unusual continuation. I proceeded along it with confidence. Here Kasparov became lost in thought for real. I had managed to unmask and use precisely those nuances of the position which Kasparov's group had failed to find.

Everything hung by a thread. The situation was acute for both sides. I was still uncertain that I had saved myself, but I knew that I could win at any moment. Then, in a display of coldbloodedness, Kasparov made three brilliant moves in a row for a beautiful draw.

This game was the best in terms of *mutual quality*. Afterward there were games in which I played well but Kasparov was not in top form, or games where he played well but I didn't. Here, though, we both turned in outstanding performances.

This game showed me a great deal; primarily, that Kasparov was not as good as he thought he was, or as good as he presented himself. He had squandered a large advantage. Moreover, he gave me chances to win. But with my time trouble, Kasparov would have been able to save himself by perpetual check, and thus my short-lived triumph was doused.

The first four games affirmed the notion that the battle would be serious and brutal. So far neither side could claim any clear superiority. I realized that I was gaining my form and that Kasparov was having trouble finding himself and getting his game on track. I believed in a favorable outcome for myself.

The next critical moments came in the eighth and ninth games. During these two games I let victory slip from my hands for the first time. This is not only my impression, however. At the conclusion of the New York battles, I spoke with two people whose stance in the match was neutral, the grand masters Robert Byrne and Jonathan Tisdall. We discussed the dramatic reversals of the match, its dynamics, the ups and downs of the fight; counted the chances missed by Kasparov and me, and came to the conclusion that the score of six to six was a gift for Kasparov. He was neither repelling my initiative nor my

constant advantage. I could have been leading by a minimum of one point, but a two-point lead would have been
more accurately in keeping with the true distribution of
strength in the first half.

I remember my conversation with Yasser Seirawan
sometime soon after my first loss. Trying to console me
and keeping in mind the circumstances in which the
match was being played, he said that if I could play out
the first half and be only one point down, he would
consider me to be one of the most brilliant of all grandmasters. A very sensitive person, he had no concept of
how one could put up with such nuisances created for
me in New York without suffering serious losses. Yet
I managed to overcome it all and still put pressure on
Kasparov.

It's a pity I couldn't press him all the way. These set-
backs occurred in the eighth and ninth games. In the
eighth game the position was adjourned with a forced
win on the board. There weren't any complexities to
speak of. It would have been sufficient to analyze them
well, understand the weaknesses, not neglect the fine
points, and everything would have led to a textbooklike
rout. But this didn't happen. It didn't happen because
our camp was off in its analysis. If a loss stands on the
board, you can't escape it no matter how much you analyze. It was not Kasparov's team's analysis but ours that
turned out to be completely superficial. I understood this
after five moves. I was deflated, certain that I had suddenly let a win slip away. But I pulled myself together
and outplayed Kasparov for the second time. Victory was
again so close! I hurried and played carelessly. Kasparov
took advantage of my lapse and forced a draw.

I have no one but myself to blame for the draw in the

ninth game. Still, I could consider the score of six to six at intermission to be a success. In Lyons, I thought, everything will be different. I'll prove myself there and not pass up my chances. Not without some satisfaction I heard how Kasparov gave a televised interview in which he complained of unluckiness and the unfairness of fate. He had had so many chances to crush me. But he hadn't played well. These provocative statements were calculated for a wider audience interested only in the result, not in the content of the games. Those who love chess and understand it saw everything in its true colors. And they believed in me—or feared for Kasparov.

From afar I had hoped that at Lyons it would be easier, that the chess atmospherics would be cleaner. But it turned out that the organization there was entirely subpar. Why that was so is difficult to say. It may have been that the organizers were in worse financial shape, but more likely the key to the problem was the careless manner in which the roles were distributed among the people responsible for this half of the match.

I must mention the circumstances in which I had to live and work in Lyons. When, on the day before the closing, Campomanes stopped by to see me in order to take care of some paperwork, I took him around to our lodgings, he was so shocked by what he saw that he couldn't speak at first. Then he said that he had never seen conditions this bad anywhere.

Objectively speaking, the house was not bad. It was cozy and maybe even sufficiently roomy for one family. Not a bad place to relax: The area was lovely, quiet, with an excellent view, very green with beautiful old trees, a swimming pool in a corner of the park nearby. It would no doubt be very pleasant here in summer. But it was winter and everything was covered with snow. The heating was erratic; either it was turned off completely or it roasted us at full blast.

Worst of all, there was essentially nowhere to work. The only places were a large living room with a fireplace on the first floor, and our bedrooms upstairs. We used the living room, but one pair of us working together would invariably disturb a second pair. Then all the other assistants would come down from their rooms to grab a bite because the dining room table, large and oval and able to accommodate the whole team, was also here. Right off the living room was the kitchen with its inescapable aromas. Even if we had stayed here for just a few days, we still wouldn't have been comfortable, but we lived in this house for almost two months. And not only lived here, but worked here as well, sometimes around the clock.

If I had won, I would probably have remembered this whole time in Lyons, including the living conditions, with gratitude and fondness. But since it turned out differently, one tends to look at everything through the prism of defeat.

Still, I shouldn't have lost the match. From one game to the next it was clear that Kasparov was playing more ponderously, becoming ever more nervous and fidgety. I, on the other hand, felt confident and strong. I saw that the scales were tipping in my favor. Toward the second half of November Kasparov was undoubtedly ripe for defeat, but, alas, I was not ready to win.

In game after game I missed opportunities to take the

lead. I did not understand what was happening. The initiative still belonged to me, and I believed that at any moment now . . .

Then came the sixteenth game. Again we did not prepare very well at home. In fact, we chose a continuation that was obviously bad. Kasparov repeated the Scotch Defense he had played successfully in the fourteenth game, and we had had the time to mull it over but, instead, we chose the worst of all evils. Kasparov, though, wasn't prepared to accept such a gift. He should have won somewhere near the thirtieth move, but he came unglued and let me slip out of a completely won position. Right before the adjournment I managed to intensify play and put myself on an equal footing. This was a minor miracle that would not have been possible without Kasparov's help.

Now I had simply to keep my head above water in order to hold to a draw. Again, our home analysis let us down. The position was very tricky, and it was difficult to say who had the better chances: White to win or Black to draw. Then it became clear that Black had a forcing draw, but I missed it. After the game Kasparov admitted that his group had not found the forcing win. Our group, I conceded, had not seen the draw.

This victory was achieved through such agony that Kasparov rejoiced in it more than any other in the entire match. But he was not rejoicing for long: My next win was decisive. From a position that did not presage any danger for Black, I made a move unforeseen by Kasparov and his position unraveled. It was play at its subtlest, play that was a present to the commentators. It was like a textbook game: I strengthened my pieces with each move while weakening my opponent's and forcing them back. There was nothing accidental in this game. True, toward the end Kasparov began to make a few moves that diluted somewhat the overall effect, but by then it was too late to fix anything.

The score in the match was tied again. Any moment now, I felt, something would happen. I realized it would take one precise jolt for my initiative to become my victory. In the next game I threw in one of my secret home preparations. I had kept it in reserve for an appropriate time since the New York half, and I put a great deal of hope in it.

I played the opening of the eighteenth game in a matter of minutes, moving in accordance with the variation worked out at home, confidently and without looking back. Why should I try to act cunning and feign deep thought? I knew that the time for that would come somewhere around the twentieth move, when Kasparov would reveal his defense. I moved and moved, and suddenly I saw a trap waiting for me. One move by Kasparov had not been taken into account by our group's analysis. The situation became hopeless. It was impossible to reverse the game's momentum.

Again I found myself in the position of having to play catch-up. It wasn't the first time in the match, but this time my mood was not the same as before: it is extremely oppressive to lose a game due to your own fault. What is there to believe in when your best weapon is smashed to smithereens?

Feeling as I did, I was unable to tie the score in the nineteenth game. Kasparov won the next game, the twentieth, and fortified his lead by two points with four remaining to play. I was facing a two-point margin with only four games left in which to tie it and move ahead!

I knew that then no one believed in me. But I knew the battle was not yet over and I set myself to fight right up to the last minute. I was lucky in that Kasparov also figured the case was closed. He even had a chance to beat me by a margin of three points—the margin he had promised. But I went at him as if nothing had happened. I played variations that I wanted to play and played them rather successfully. In three games I had real chances to win, but only once was I able to realize it. The battle was tense up to the last moment. In the final game, half an hour before the end, I was standing on the brink of a win. I saw that I had a win. All I had to do was make several precise moves and the score would be tied again, just as in the last match three years ago in Seville, twelve to twelve. I still had to play and play very delicately in a very sharp position to carry this game out to a win. But I was already in the grip of the win, I was already experiencing it when I committed an irreparably gross error. In one moment I had let go of everything I had so assuredly held in my hands: a win in the game and a draw in the match. I still clutched at illusory straws, but it was over. No more chances! No more! It was all over!

I lost the match. I blame only myself for this. There were many opportunities to win. But I missed them, no one else.

Yet, in many ways, my old confidence has returned. In the previous match with Kasparov, for instance, I always feared playing Black, but now this feeling has disappeared. It is a pleaure to see that this confidence has been transferred to my team as well.

Now I am faced with a new ascent.

INDEX